FORGIVENESS EMBRACED

HOW TO KNOW IF YOU HAVE REALLY FORGIVEN
WHAT TO DO IF YOU HAVEN'T

An Inquiry Into How Joseph, The Patriarch,
Lost A Coat And Inherited A Kingdom
DAVID D. KING, ThD, PhD

Great care has been taken in this work to ensure accuracy in use of language, grammar, syntax, and punctuation. When such errors were perceived or found within the quoted research material, those errors were retained as they were found in their published manuscripts by the authors of origin.

Because of the dynamic nature of the Internet, any web addresses or links contained in this book may have changed since publication and may no longer be valid.

The views expressed in this work are solely those of the author and do not necessarily reflect the views of the publisher. The publisher hereby disclaims any responsibility for said views of the author.

All Scripture quotations are taken from *The New International Version of The Holy Bible* unless otherwise noted. © Copyright 1973, 1978, 1984, 2011, Biblica (Worldwide)
NIV refers to The New International Version of the Bible
KJV refers to The King James Version of the Bible
NASB refers to The New American Standard Bible
NLT refers to the New Living Translation of the Bible

Title: Forgiveness Embraced
Sub Title: How To Know If You Have Really Forgiven
What To Do If You Haven't

Publisher: Mission Supply Service cc
Edited by: Jane Mqamelo
Typesetting and Cover Design by: Lauren Burger

First Edition 2017
ISBN – 978-1-9732243-0-3

Mission Supply Services, Cape Town, RSA

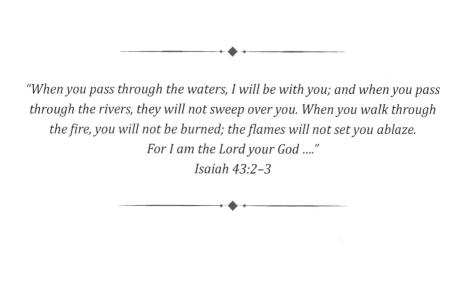

"When you pass through the waters, I will be with you; and when you pass through the rivers, they will not sweep over you. When you walk through the fire, you will not be burned; the flames will not set you ablaze.
For I am the Lord your God ...."
Isaiah 43:2–3

CONTENTS

Dedication i

Foreword. iii

Preface iv

Acknowledgements. vi

Introduction. 1

CHAPTER ONE
Joseph's Defining Moments In A Dysfunctional Family 16

CHAPTER TWO
Joseph's Defining Moments In A Demoralizing Fix 31

CHAPTER THREE
Joseph's Defining Moments In Another Domestic Fiasco 42

CHAPTER FOUR
Joseph's Defining Moments In A Detention Facility 58

CHAPTER FIVE
Joseph's Defining Moments As A Distinguished Financier 81

CHAPTER SIX
Joseph's Defining Moments In Displaying Forgiveness 92

CHAPTER SEVEN
Joseph's Defining Moment: Embracing His Delighted Father . . . 119

CONCLUSION
When Forgiveness Is Embraced, Grace Abounds 132

Bibliography 151

About The Author 156

DEDICATION

They say it is customary to write a dedication page. While I admit there are many people to whom I could and should dedicate this work because of their love, devotion and support of me and my ministry over the years, I feel led of the Lord to take this dedication in an unusual direction. I trust that those I spoke of will understand and know of my love and gratitude for them. Please allow me a little unorthodoxy in the dedication.

I dedicate this to all of you who read this book and fall into one, two, three, or all four of these following categories: a) those who find it hard to forgive themselves, b) those who have longed to receive forgiveness from someone they hurt – but forgiveness has not been granted, (c) those who need to extend forgiveness to someone but just cannot or will not – or think they have extended it, but they do not live a life exhibiting forgiveness, and (d) those of us who need to learn that embracing forgiveness is a life-long assignment that we must choose to do every single day that we live. I guess that is all of us.

Finally, I am certain that we all know someone in our past who has had an unhealthy outlook on forgiveness. Perhaps that person had been hurt, and now their philosophy is, "When a person hurts me, that's it. I'm done with them. I won't give them the time of day. Write them off! Move on!" It is possible we have all been that way at one time or another. I also suspect we have been in each of these categories, and there may have been times when we were in all categories at the same time.

If by chance (or divine intervention – however you perceive it), you have picked up this book for a casual read, I hope you will read further. I do not say this in a condemning or castigating spirit, because again, we have either all been there or we are there. But if this describes you, I am glad you're here. I am dedicating this book to you and to whatever God chooses to do in your future and in your relationships.

Yes, think of that one person that this book could be for. It is for them. Maybe it is for you. I know this has been for me. May we all learn together and may the Holy Spirit teach us.

In addition, I dedicate this work to my darling wife, Dr. Carie Suzanne Tucker King. More than her expertise as a university professor and a communications expert *par excellance*, I am appreciative of her unconditional love. While authoring her own book, her support for me to complete this work kept me going. I love you, *my Carie*.

FOREWORD

Forgiveness Embraced is a fascinating book written by a challenging and provocative new author, David D. King, ThD, PhD.

Dr. King has provided us with a stunning and insightful analysis on the subject of forgiveness as exemplified by the Genesis account of the life of Joseph. It is a sad tale of diabolical maltreatment and servitude. But what man intended for evil, God intended for good. Dr. King opens his book with a devastating experience as challenging as any in the story he so carefully weaves of Joseph and his band of brothers. In the dead of night, a phone call changed David's life forever. His heart was turned inside out as he learned that his two adult children lay injured among the crumpled remains of auto glass and steel. They survived, but dreams were diminished, hopes crashed, and futures crippled.

On his forgiveness journey, Dr. King deals with his own humanness and the multiple "whys" that are so deeply personal. Forgiveness? Who could extend it, much less embrace it, at such a time as this?

Joseph, the beloved boy with a coat of many colors, was betrayed by his brothers, forsaken, sold into slavery, and presumed dead. But God ... (don't you love that?) But God steps in and changes the narrative. We see how various people react to His grace, leading to human forgiveness.

Dr. King guides us through a journey fraught with life-altering challenges. We learn of priceless and healing acts of forgiveness which will work in our everyday and inevitable realities. The Genesis story is beautifully complemented by the interpretations, comments and illustrations of a broad array of other authors. It is a rich and rewarding read. I commend to you this offering of spiritual truth and life. God bless you, David, for your consummate commitment over the years in bringing this grace-based message of hope, liberation and ultimate freedom through forgiveness – forgiveness of ourselves, forgiveness toward others, and (as unthinkable as it may seem) our forgiveness of God.

Dr. Robert Jeffress, Senior Pastor, First Baptist Church, Dallas, Texas
Teacher, Pathway to Victory, FOX News Contributor

PREFACE

The phone had that chilling ring. You know the kind I'm talking about – the kind of ring that says something isn't right ... and the voice on the other end confirmed my speculation; this would not end well. What had been a good day had now turned sour. Who could know, on that chilly October night, returning home after preaching at the church I pastored, that our world would never be the same again?

The two oldest children, living three and a half hours away, had been in a life-threatening car accident and airlifted to a trauma unit. Their lives hung in the balance. I knew that if we did not make the trip that night, we might never get the opportunity again.

To cut a long story short, they survived; the oldest one now with permanent brain damage and living in a care facility. Needless to say, it is not what a father dreams of for his (then) twenty-four year old daughter who had been living on her own and planning for marriage. Due to physical and psychological injuries sustained, our son's dream of a military career was over. I'm sure you can imagine that God and I had a few unusual conversations to say the least. I was not all right with this.

God brought us all through those difficult days only to prove that I was not capable of coming through that tragedy on my own. How I continued to preach through that nightmare was a miracle in itself. I felt the prayers of God's dear and faithful people, but I walked in a daze for months, wondering what had happened. I was angry and bitter but tried to keep it hidden on the inside. There would be even more challenges ahead.

Thankfully, I came to the point where forgiveness could find its way into my heart. Wait a minute: *forgiveness*? Can someone actually forgive God? Is that even possible? Not exactly, as we will discuss later. In fact, I asked God for forgiveness. I came to discover that God was not asking my permission for anything or my forgiveness for feeling that I had been dealt a bad hand. He was asking for my trust and obedience. I would be lying to you if I said it was easy. As one caring pastor reminded me: "David, God did not cause this, but He is working through a process in your life that will be to your children's good, your good, and to His glory. Let Him!" I believe that to be true, but I certainly wish He had done it some other way.

I tell this story because it is what brings me to this book. These personal circumstances will not be dealt with in this study, but embracing forgiveness will be. All of us, regardless of who we are or where we come from, have a story to tell, and we have all had to deal with forgiveness in some fashion. Either you forgave or needed to be forgiven. Perhaps you have sat on both sides of the fence, maybe even more than once.

In the Scriptures we are told to forgive. I am thankful, however, that the Lord does not leave us there with that commandment. We are not only told to forgive, but the Scriptures walk us through a process; they display forgiveness for us, and then they authenticate for us what real, embraced forgiveness looks like as seen in many Biblical personalities – none greater than Jesus of course, but also in a man named Joseph from the Old Testament. Apart from Jesus Christ, this man intrigues me like no other in the history of the human race. As we see in the life of this great patriarch, God's Word demonstrates and authenticates for us that forgiveness really is possible, although you might have thought differently. Furthermore, the Scriptures show us that forgiveness will not be an overnight process. In fact, the experience of genuine forgiveness is only for those who embrace its life-long assignment. Yes, you heard me right – life-long. Trust me: you will not complete this process tonight. Don't even expect to. But certainly, begin it tonight!

Dear One, in whatever you may pass through, I hope you will feel the presence of the Lord Jesus and the power of the Holy Spirit guiding you every step of the way, and that when forgiveness is needed, in whatever circumstance, you will eventually embrace it.

DAVID KING

ACKNOWLEDGEMENTS

I would like to acknowledge a few of the people who have helped me through the process of the initial research which eventually led to this book. For the phone conversations, emails, advice and editing, my sincere thanks.

My older sister, Cathi King Warren, proofread the original version before this book was born. It was originally my doctoral dissertation. I am grateful for her love and how she used her God-given talents in support of the original version of this work.

I would also like to acknowledge the work of Dr. David A. Keeny, Dean of Biblical Studies for Louisiana Baptist University and my dissertation chair. As previously stated, the inspiration for this book was born out of my dissertation for my Ph.D. Dr. Keeny's insight was helpful in guiding me through the process. The original form of this book was quite different than what you now see. The material you hold in your hands was reformatted and converted from a research project into this book form in order to make it available to you. My thanks to Dr. Keeny.

For the tireless edit work of Jane Mqamelo and the printing work done under the direction of Stefan and Unda Loots of Mission Supply Services of Cape Town, South Africa, I am forever grateful. May God continue to bless your work.

I am grateful for the CEO and Founder of Harvesters Ministries, Steven Loots, and his wife Hannalie. It was Steven who urged me to complete this book. Thank you for the partnership in the ministry that we share. And finally, in virtually every step of my ministry – from my ordination, which he preached, until today – spanning some 30 years – there has been a lifelong mentor, friend, confidante, and encourager without whom I would not be who I am. I owe a special gratitude to him for his love and support in good times and tough times. He has cheered me on and cried with me. He also contributed to some of the editing of the original work of this book ...

... that would be my uncle, Dr. Ted S. Roe. I love you, Uncle Ted!

INTRODUCTION

Is embracing forgiveness a good thing? The affirmative is the obvious answer to that question (in a perfect world) unless you are the one who must render the treatment. If the old adage is true that "to err is human; to forgive divine", then for humans to forgive must be diabolically toilsome and painful. First, forgiveness implies that something went wrong in a relationship. Something happened that should not have happened, and consequently, a broken heart was unavoidable. Second, forgiveness is rarely executed by the trespasser. Third, forgiveness is most often executed by the one who has been trespassed against.

History is replete with stories of forgiveness, stories read about but rarely experienced to the extent of some events that we will explore. I invite you to gather around some of these narratives, mainly from Genesis, chapters 37–50. Pay close attention to the traumatic events and allow yourself to be introspective.

Before beginning with events in the Bible, I want to show you a description of forgiveness from author Michael Henderson. He writes about forgiveness in nations, communities, and political regimes of man's inhumanity to man. In his book entitled *Forgiveness: Breaking the Chain of Hate,* he addresses encounters in a chapter that he titles "From Grini to Gulag." Henderson recounts the chilling details:

> Father Lawrence Jenco, from the Servite Order, was working in a relief agency in Lebanon when he was taken hostage. As he stepped from a car in Rome within days of his release from captivity, a photographer shouted at him from a distance, "Father Jenco, what are your feelings towards the terrorists who held you?"
>
> He responded without much thought: "I am a Christian. I must forgive them." The sentiment had been in his heart from some time. "I had come to understand that my captors could not be my enemies. They had to be my brothers. Through his life and through his final agony, Jesus taught us that

the heart of love is forgiveness. This is what he asked of us. This is what he asked of me during my captivity." In some ways, Father Jenco found it harder to forgive what he felt was inadequate responses to his plight by the U.S. government and his church than he did the cruelty of his captors. "Having forgiven," he says, "I am liberated. I need no longer be determined by the past."

Toward the end of Jenco's captivity, one of his guards, a man named Sayeed who had at times brutalized him, sat down on the mat with him. He had recently started calling him Abouna, an Arabic name meaning dear father. At first he was "Jenco," then "Lawrence," then Abouna, indicating by the change of voice that the change of heart was taking place. Sayeed asked if Jenco remembered the first six months of his captivity. Jenco responded, "Yes, Sayeed. I remember all the pain and suffering you caused me and my brothers." Then Sayeed asked, "Abouna, do you forgive me?"

In his book *Bound to Forgive*, Jenco records his response:

These quietly spoken words overwhelmed me. As I sat blindfolded, unable to see the man who had been my enemy, I understood I was called to forgive, to let go of the revenge, retaliation, and forgive.

And I was challenged to forgive him unconditionally. I could not forgive him on the condition that he change his behavior to conform to my wishes or values. I had no control over his response. I understood I was to say yes.

I said, "Sayeed, there were times I hated you. I was filled with anger and revenge for what you did to me and my brothers. But Jesus said on a mountain top that I was not to hate you. I was to love you. Sayeed, I need to ask God's forgiveness and yours."[1]

---

1   Lawrence Jenco, *Bound to Forgive* (Notre Dame, IN: Ave Maria Press, 1995) pages 13–14, quoted in Michael Henderson, *Forgiveness: Breaking the Chain of Hate* (Wilsonville, Oregon: Book Partners, Inc., 1999), 130–131.

How does that kind of forgiveness happen? In every generation, the issue of forgiveness has touched all human beings. No person has ever lived who has not had to deal with this in some way. Whether forgiving or being forgiven, this issue is a great touchstone of civilization that transcends all cultural boundaries. If I decide to live life without forgiveness, that one decision destroys the very core and inner soul of who God made me and intended me to be. Therefore, this human dynamic of forgiveness begs for my attention as a Christian. It is essential for healing throughout all aspects of my life.

Apart from Jesus Christ, seldom is there found in Scripture a person who demonstrates the dynamics of forgiveness better than Joseph. In Genesis 37–50, we see that Joseph has learned some things we need to observe. Marvin Jones speaks about the integrity and the character of this man Joseph. He writes, "The true test of Joseph's character is not in his leadership abilities, not in his administrative abilities but in his willingness to forgive his brothers who had mistreated and abused him."[2] On the surface, this would appear accurate since Scripture bears out this fact regarding Joseph, but what about the things that are not read regarding his character? Maybe what speaks the loudest is that which is not said about this eventual patriarch.

Allow me to introduce Joseph's father, Jacob. Jacob came from a dysfunctional family himself. You may recall that as a deceiver, Jacob stole his brother's birthright. Later, Jacob married Leah, but he really wanted to marry Rachel. He later married Rachel, and both wives had handmaidens who bore sons of Jacob. Dysfunctional, isn't it? At any rate, the most common belief about the birth order of Jacob's sons goes as follows:

Name	Mother	Scriptural authority
Reuben	Leah	Genesis 29:32
Simeon	Leah	Genesis 29:33
Levi	Leah	Genesis 29:34

---

2   Marvin D. Jones, *Joseph, a Man of Integrity: A Homiletical Approach* (Cluj-Napoca, Cluj, Romania: Emanuel University Press, 2008), 114.

Name	Mother	Scriptural authority
Judah	Leah	Genesis 29:35
Dan	Bilhah (Rachel's handmaid)	Genesis 30:5–6
Naphtali	Bilhah (Rachel's handmaid)	Genesis 30:7–8
Gad	Zilpah (Leah's handmaid)	Genesis 30:10–11
Asher	Zilpah (Leah's handmaid)	Genesis 30:12–13
Issachar	Leah	Genesis 30:17–18
Zebulun	Leah	Genesis 30:19–20
Joseph	Rachel	Genesis 30:23–24
Benjamin	Rachel	Genesis 35:16–18

Only one daughter whom we know of was born to Jacob, and her name was Dinah. Dinah was born to Leah, after Zebulun and before Joseph. Joseph was not Jacob's firstborn, but he was Jacob's firstborn of Rachel, and this may have caused the favoritism. We do know that Joseph was Jacob's favorite. As we will see, this proved troublesome for this family, to say the least.

Joseph's wisdom in the matter of, *"... but God intended it for good ..."* (Gen. 50:20) transcends cultures and generations, and it reaches us today through the thousands of years since Joseph's words were first uttered. The fact that Joseph, figuratively, exchanges his coat for a kingdom makes me wonder, "Joseph, what did you know that mankind has yet to discover?"

Furthermore, the life of Joseph paints a beautiful portrait of God's providential will, love, forgiveness, mercy, and grace albeit at an awfully high price. And if it is felt that the price of having God's favor is too high, one only needs to count the cost of not having His favor. The life of Joseph truly shouts for our attention.

To embrace forgiveness – is it really possible? What makes this so difficult? Forgiveness is not a tangible thing. In other words, it is not something we can visibly see, hear, touch, taste, or smell. Yet the effects of forgiveness can be seen, heard, and felt. Since it is invisible and is more of a state of the heart, how can we be certain we have completely forgiven others, thus being made emotionally and psychologically whole?

Through the seasons of Joseph's life, many things will be discovered about personal and family dysfunction, jealousy, preparation, leadership, the sovereignty of God, guilt, repentance, redemption, and blessing – and above all else, leaving those earthly coats behind for a Godly kingdom; such things are part of the forgiving process.

Initially, we must understand that what happened to Joseph was not a random set of circumstances. You cannot consider that he had just a stroke of "bad luck." He was not a man who was just "down and out." On the contrary, Joseph was a man whom God had hand-picked for a purpose.

If you should see anything similar here to your own life, think it not coincidental. We are no different, although our circumstances vary dramatically. God has chosen each one of us for His tasks, and He allows you and me to go through circumstances that build character in order to strengthen our resolve so that we might better serve Him. When we grow to the point of being able to forgive, it is part of the process orchestrated by God.

That said, should it be assumed that God *caused* these bad things to happen to Joseph? Definitely not. In fact, Joseph rhetorically answers this in chapters 45 and 50 in his dealings with his brothers. He clearly enunciates God's part in what happened when he says, *"You intended to harm me, but God intended it for good to accomplish what is now being done, the saving of many lives"* (Gen. 50:20).

This raises a question that probably has no answer: Had Joseph's brothers never committed such evil, would it still have been God's plan to send Joseph to Egypt in order to prepare for the family to come at a later time? Might Joseph have found an advertisement in the *Canaan Daily Times* looking for a Prime Minister in Egypt, and then sent his résumé over by courier? Doubtful, but one never knows how God could have worked out the details. This is certain: God is capable of orchestrating even the most difficult set of circumstances in order to accomplish His perfect will — even with us.

The series of events that we will discuss in this book do occur as the result of unfortunate misbehavior, blatant disregard for human life and a desire on the part of Jacob's boys to see their brother – their own flesh and blood – killed. They had planned his murder in cold blood. Had it not been for Reuben and Judah's half-hearted and impure motivation for wanting to spare Joseph's life, and had it not been for the providential hand of God upon Joseph's life, this deadly deed would probably have been carried out. It is safe to conclude that most of Joseph's brothers wanted to see his life extinguished.

It must be obvious at this point (although this will be further explored) that these boys were troublesome. We often make the mistake today of thinking that because this story is "in the Bible" that these were good men who only made a mistake. Nothing could be further from the truth. These were bad men, steeped in a dysfunction that dated back even further than the days of their grandfather and great-grandfather, and this entire scenario smacks of the unsettled days of the Wild West in America.

Be not mistaken however, a *Bonanza* story will not be found here (a TV Western series that aired from 1959 to 1973 on the American TV network, NBC, and still runs in syndication to this day). There is no Ben Cartwright with his nurturing sons, Adam, Hoss, and Little Joe, caring for one another while trying to survive at the base of the beautiful hills near Lake Tahoe, cultivating the family's six hundred thousand acre ranch, *Ponderosa*, shooting bad guys and solving all their social problems in a one-hour time frame – not in this story! These are Jacob's sons, full of primitive dysfunction and jealousy. They are so packed with explosive hatred that, if given the chance, they would willingly kill – not just to protect themselves, but in order to obtain what they desired and to cover up their bad choices.

Why do we need to study the life of Joseph? The story is so familiar, is it really worth the time? What would cause you to sit down and look once again at such a drama from the Old Testament, and why did God include this in the Canon of Scripture? Probably one of the best reasons for this inquiry is to examine mankind's tendencies. Our humanity hardly varies from that of Scripture's characters, although culturally we are removed quite a bit. Hearts become broken. Emotions are easily damaged. Lives become spiritually and psychologically wrecked, and even Christians can crumble under the weight of such strain. As a result, we are left feeling abused, mistreated and abandoned. Whether justified or perceived reality, we often find our heart debating this issue of forgiveness: "Is it right to forgive?" "What about trying again?" "Is it safe to be vulnerable this time?"

In examining Joseph's life, not only will forgiveness begin to emerge, but what we will see is a process. Joseph was not ready to forgive his brothers the moment he was thrown into the pit. Yet fast-forward to another day and time, in a different country, after years of maturity and under a different set of circumstances, we see the new Joseph, unlike the one we knew before.

Was Joseph just a boy with a sweet disposition? Was he someone whom we might say had the emotional make-up to forgive easily? Was he just born that way? That could have been the case, but probably not. There is more reason to believe that at this stage of his life, Joseph was egocentric, selfish, naive, arrogant and immature. As this story progresses, nothing less will be seen than a man who undergoes a total transformation wrought by the Holy Spirit. Note that God is working in Joseph through his own family dysfunctions while in adversarial situations with his brothers, while being sold (possibly twice), while working for a man who had a domestic challenge of his own to deal with, and then while in prison. And even in prison, there was a specific circumstance that happened which makes one wonder if at that point he still was not ready for greatness. No, Joseph was not prepared to meet his brothers until the day he finally saw them. What would have happened had Joseph encountered them before his heart was transformed? Thanks be to God, we will never know.

The Old Testament rarely displays a panoramic scene so vivid and so relevant to each individual as this story of Joseph. Never has there been a time when any person, whether saved or unsaved, has not had to deal with forgiveness in some measure.

Yet why deal with forgiveness? Isn't there something within each of us that cries for justice? Or, wouldn't it be easier to just ignore those who have

done us wrong and hope they fade off into the sunset and out of our lives?
It might seem that way, but as David Stoop interestingly assesses, it is not
that easy.

> The Journey along the Path of Forgiveness isn't easy. In many ways
> it will feel like an uphill climb. It goes against the grain in so many
> ways. How much easier it is simply to say, "Let them pay! They did
> the wrong!" When we take the Path of Forgiveness, however, we
> repudiate revenge and let go of our desire to get even. Forgiveness
> requires that we accept the undeserved. Even though it isn't fair,
> that's what Jesus expects us to do." [3]

"... we repudiate revenge ..." Don't you love Stoop's phrase? I do.
Repudiating revenge is rarely heard of in this culture. The heartbeat
of every unregenerate soul (and many regenerate ones) is to justify
vengeance and to right the wrongs.

Before answering the question of why people should forgive, let us
view an illustration given from Dr. Robert Jeffress as he speculates what
might have happened had Joseph not extended forgiveness:

> Imagine that when his (Joseph's) brothers came requesting grain,
> Joseph had answered, "You want food? Funny you should mention
> that. Just today I was thinking about how much I wanted food when
> you left me for dead in that stinking pit."
>
> Had Joseph held on to his desire for vengeance and allowed his
> brothers to starve to death, the lasting consequences would have
> reverberated throughout eternity. Instead, Joseph's remarkable
> story not only ensured the development of the nation of Israel,
> from whom Jesus Christ would come to save the world, but also
> serves as an inspiration and illustration for how we're to bestow
> true forgiveness upon others. [4]

---

3   David Stoop, *Forgiving the Unforgivable* (Ann Arbor, MI: Vine Books,
     Servant Publications, 2001),100.

4   Robert Jeffress, *When Forgiveness Doesn't Make Sense* (Colorado Springs,
     CO: Waterbrook Press, 2000), 171.

All of this brings me to several reasons to forgive. I suppose there are many considerations too numerous to mention, so I offer only five brief reasons or thoughts on why we should forgive, not necessarily listed in any order of importance:

I. FORGIVENESS IS NECESSARY BECAUSE GOD IS UP TO SOMETHING.

Jeffress was alluding to this very thing. God had something better in mind. God was busy orchestrating the events whereby redemption would one day be complete, and He was not going to allow these boys, who would later be patriarchs and catalysts for the twelve tribes of Israel, to stand in His way. The potential to derail and thwart God's agenda was inbred in these boys, and to add fuel to the flame, it is certain that Satan was doing his very best to wreck the whole plan. Nevertheless, God was at work. For many years while in Egypt, Joseph's heart was undergoing some much-needed repairs.

When you and I are tempted to ask why we should forgive, it behooves us to be cognizant of the fact that God is up to something, and all of what He is doing has not yet been revealed. God is up to something!

II. FORGIVENESS IS NECESSARY BECAUSE HEALING IS NEEDED.

God is working through a process to provide healing. Dr. R.T. Kendall, Pastor Emeritus of Westminster Chapel of London, has done extensive counseling, research and writing in this area of forgiveness. Some of his work will be examined further in later chapters. What instigated Kendall's research in this area was not the fact that he is a scholar, although he is. It was not to write a book, although a book was born as a result. His research was simply birthed out of the pangs of his own experience – in needing to forgive certain people. Whether those people ever asked for forgiveness is uncertain, but Kendall concludes in his writings that God put him through a process, the result of which provided true healing.

In many of Kendall's books he elaborates on this healing, but specifically in *Total Forgiveness* he says the offended is the one who needs the healing.

> Not everyone we must forgive is an enemy. There are those we must forgive who either do not know they have hurt us or, if they do, would never have done so intentionally. But we must forgive anyone for whom we feel anger because it is we, not they, who are in need of healing. That is why total forgiveness – in a sense – becomes a selfish thing.[5]

Kendall further expounds that the offended needs mercy and forgiveness as well. In other words, I ought to want to extend it to others because it is the very thing that I need for myself. No doubt there have been times after someone has hurt you that you have thought, "Well, they just need help. They are a piece of work! They have issues in their lives that they need to deal with." Right or wrong, this is certain: Everyone needs healing.

III. FORGIVENESS IS NEEDED BECAUSE RECONCILIATION WITH OTHERS IS A MUST.

You and I were created to live with many distinctive qualities, not the least of which is to live in community and to be in unity with all men and women. It would seem at times that this is impossible, but this is what God has commanded of His children. The Apostle Paul said, *"If it is possible, as far as it depends on you, live at peace with everyone"* (Rom. 12:18).

If we Christians are to experience life in all the fullness that God intended and be filled with the Holy Spirit, we must be right with our fellow man, in so far as it is possible. In so far as it is *not* possible, we must let God assess those circumstances and allow Him to render the findings as He desires and move on. Yet an attempt to be unified with one another is essential, and this applies to those inside our households as well as those outside.

IV. FORGIVENESS IS NEEDED FOR RECONCILIATION WITH GOD.

Remember the question I posed in the Preface? "Is it necessary to forgive God? Is it even possible?" Whether or not it is necessary might

---

5   R.T. Kendall, *Total Forgiveness* (Lake Mary, FL: Charisma House, 2002), 2-3.

not even be the issue. There is not one shred of evidence found in the Scriptures that indicates we can forgive God. There may be instances, such as in the book of Job, where a person has issues and quarrels with God (and who of us has not?). Yet even Job came to realize that what God does is right, and when things go wrong, God is just and fair in His dealings.

No human being can render forgiveness to God because God has no need to be forgiven of anything. However, when trauma or traumatic situations are experienced, there may be some internal healing that comes to our soul when we commune with God letting Him know of our displeasure of such outcomes. At times it may be helpful for me to say, "God, I know You do not need or desire my forgiveness for what has happened, but I accept whatever You want to do in this situation. I realize that whatever bad or evil things that have happened, You did not cause them. You have allowed them and You are in control of working out the details for my good and for Your ultimate glory. I don't like what has happened, but I trust You!" Sometimes after heart-wrenching and excruciatingly painful experiences, a conversation with God leading us to that conclusion is valuable to the healing process.

Another aspect to being reconciled with God is the sequence of forgiveness that must take place; it is only possible to be reconciled to God after we have been reconciled to one another.

Jesus said, *"Therefore, if you are offering your gift at the altar and there remember that your brother or sister has something against you, leave your gift there in front of the altar. First go and be reconciled to them; then come and offer your gift"* (Matthew 5:23–24). The offender is to leave the gift and "high-tail it" back to the offended.

Have you ever thought about this? This is the only time in Scripture where we are told to *not* give a gift to the Lord right away. We are to leave it at the altar, implying that the gift is partially given, but not totally given yet. Then we are to go and make things right with the brother. Only after that has been accomplished to best of our ability may we return and offer our gift to the Lord. In other words, Jesus lays out a process for His people to be reconciled with one another and He commands it to be done. He implies that believers are wrong if they think they can be right with God while having problems among one other. Consequently, this could be one of the greatest reasons for embracing forgiveness – because you and I desperately need to be reconciled to God.

V. FORGIVENESS IS NEEDED FOR RECONCILIATION WITH ONE'S SELF.

Often, the hardest person to forgive is yourself. For many, it is often easier to forgive someone else than to forgive themselves when they are dealing with guilt and shame. In fact, the closer a person is to someone, the harder it is to forgive that person. People who have no connection to one another might mistreat each other, but because of the lack of connection, it is easy to get over. Let that person, however, be a close friend or even a spouse, and it becomes much harder. Emotions run deeper when people love one another.

In like fashion, we are very close to our own being, and when something negative happens that was self-inflicted, we often desire to incarcerate ourselves into living a life without parole from guilt, shame and self-loathing, even after having the certainty of God's extended forgiveness. We are hard on ourselves. After repenting of sin and receiving God's forgiveness, we would do well to note the insights given by Counselor Mark Cosgrove in advice to fellow counselors:

> Many great sinners in the Bible found themselves accepted and forgiven by God, much to their surprise. And our counselees are to have the same forgiving attitude toward themselves. This does not mean that they will not feel terrible remorse at sin and its consequences. But they are not to look at themselves with hate, anger, or loathing. Sin is something terrible, but love is something greater. They have to forgive the past, and concentrate on the future no matter how many past failures they have.

In learning to forgive themselves they must learn to avoid the countless, self-punishing messages that they might be sending to themselves every day. [6]

When we do not forgive ourselves, it paralyzes us and prevents us from being able to live in victory on a daily basis. Furthermore, this can have a devastating effect, not only on ourselves, but on our usefulness in Kingdom work and Kingdom living, thus having a "trickle-down effect" in preventing us from building strong and healthy relationships.

Notice that the further we delve into this study of Jacob's troubled sons, the more we see of our troubled, contemporary society. An old gospel song that is hardly remembered anymore, said, "From glory to glory He leads me on, from grace to grace every day." Yet look where the Church is heading today. She should be moving on from glory to glory and victory to victory. Sad to say, this is a far cry from reality. The Church today often finds herself going from crisis to crisis, from fight to fight, from argument to argument, and from split to split.

Chuck Swindoll uses an illustration of this in his book entitled *Laugh Again* as he quotes Karen Mains relating a story.

In a parable she entitles, *A Brawling Bride,* Karen Mains paints a vivid scene, describing a suspenseful moment in a wedding ceremony. Down front stands the groom in a spotless tuxedo – handsome, smiling, full of anticipation, shoes shined, every hair in place, anxiously awaiting the presence of his bride. All attendants are in place, looking joyful and attractive. The magical moment finally arrives as the pipe organ reaches full crescendo and the stately wedding march begins.

Everyone rises and looks toward the door for their first glimpse of the bride. Suddenly there is a horrified gasp. The wedding party is shocked. The groom stares in embarrassed disbelief. Instead of a lovely woman dressed in elegant white, smiling behind a lace veil, the bride is limping down the aisle. Her dress is soiled and torn. Her leg seems twisted. Ugly cuts and bruises cover her bare arms.

---

6   Mark P. Cosgrove, *Counseling for Anger* (Dallas, TX: Word, 1988), 146-147.

Her nose is bleeding, one eye is purple and swollen, and her hair is disheveled.

"Does not this handsome groom deserve better than this?" asks the author. And then the clincher: "Alas, His bride, THE CHURCH, has been fighting again." [7]

Is that not the picture of the Bride of Christ in the twenty-first century? Does not her Groom deserve better?

Hence the reason for this study: Joseph and his family so parallel our families today. Homes are in disarray and their occupants' dresses are tattered and spoiled. Is there a quick fix? Is it possible that in this fast-paced, high-speed internet, "broad-banded," smart-phoned society where we live that answers can be found and obtained as fast as they can be downloaded? Hardly. The problems that brought the Church and society to this point did not happen overnight, and they will not be solved by tomorrow evening.

Forgiveness, as alluded to, is not something that we can attain with a credit card, coming with a complete-satisfaction, money-back guarantee. It is invisible. It cannot be seen, although the effects certainly can be seen. It is ethereal. It cannot be touched, although it must be embraced, and it is heavenly when its embrace is experienced.

Furthermore, those who know forgiveness best know that they have experienced it and extended it *over a lifetime* of situations. Consider Joseph: He may not have been very forgiving while crying in the pit that his brothers put him in and after being stripped of his patrimonial coat. Yet he embraced forgiveness from a genuine heart – granted, years later, as he exchanged that coat and found the scepter and robe of a different Kingdom.

---

7   Karen Mains, *The Key to a Loving Heart* (Elgin, IL: David C. Cook, 1979) 143-144, quoted in Charles R. Swindoll, *Laugh Again* (Dallas, TX: Word, 1992), 175.

So what challenges you in this study? What will be your greatest desire when you conclude these pages? Might these be some probing questions: Are you willing to have God's favor and at what price? What about the earthly coats you often desire and wear (figuratively speaking)? What if you were called to give those up in order to obtain God's favor – are you willing? Is it "game on" for you?

Even Christians cringe at the thought of giving up rights and personal property in the name of embracing forgiveness and finding God's favor. Jesus makes it very clear that *"whoever finds their life will lose it, and whoever loses their life for My sake will find it"* (Matt. 10:39).

Until we are willing to pay the high price of being submerged in God's purpose, we will never find the life we are looking for. But when we are willing to give up those earthly coats, allowing our hearts to go through the process of being stripped of them – and even, for a period, being placed by the enemy into a pit – one day, on the other side of victory, through patience and perseverance, a Kingdom that God has waiting for us will welcome us home.

So, my invitation to you is to read further. But Reader, beware: You enter at your own risk, for the results of our time here together might be life-changing. The things we will discover are intended to strip the child of God of his or her multi-colored dream coat, which could be somewhat humbling. It has been for me. Yet a long time ago, I heard someone say something that I have never forgotten. The only part I have forgotten is who said it, but here are the words: "If we are not willing to be humbled, we may end up being humiliated." Join me as we observe one family that unfortunately learned this the hard way.

CHAPTER ONE

JOSEPH'S DEFINING MOMENTS IN A DYSFUNCTIONAL FAMILY

Before we begin, I urge you to read Genesis 37–50. Since embracing forgiveness is a process, we need to observe all that Joseph experienced prior to extending forgiveness.

Once you have dwelt on Joseph's story in God's Word, I am sure you will agree with me that forgiveness is a process that begins with *negative circumstances,* leading us either toward eventual forgiveness or away from it, depending on the direction we choose. In this chapter, we deal primarily with one of those negative occurrences – jealousy in Jacob's family.

When Joseph is introduced to us in Genesis 37, he is with his brothers feeding the flock of his father, and he is not yet aware (or at least we are not told he is) that forgiveness will be a quality he will need to develop, embrace and extend throughout his life. In examining the life of Joseph, one almost wants to ask the question, "God, has something gone terribly wrong?" As I read the passage, I immediately discern that many details have not been recorded, but when the whole story is absorbed, it becomes obvious where God wants Joseph to be stationed. We know that story well, but it initially appears as if he is blown off course, and it would be easy for the casual onlooker to wonder if God is still in control. However, as we grasp the story in its entirety, God's plans become clearer.

Despite appearances, God is clearly at work in Joseph's life. Through events that were certainly not pleasant for Joseph, God gets him to the precise place and position where he is needed to save not just his adopted country, but his family and the Hebrew people from starvation; and it is these people, the Hebrews, from whom the Messiah will eventually emerge. There is no question that God is directing the affairs of Joseph's life and the Hebrew people at large.

When Stephen in the New Testament defends himself against the Sanhedrin, he refers to God's hand on Joseph as a given: *"Because the patriarchs were jealous of Joseph, they sold him as a slave into Egypt. But God was with him..."* (Acts 7:9). Throughout his ordeals, God at no point forsakes Joseph.

When we read through the Old Testament, we discover that there is more said about Joseph than any other Old Testament figure. In rather colorful language, Chuck Swindoll bears this fact out.

No one who does a serious study of Joseph's life would deny that he was a great man. And yet he never accomplished any of the things we normally associate with biblical greatness. He never slew a giant. He never wrote a line of Scripture or made any vast prophetic predictions like Daniel. Come to think of it, Joseph never even performed a single miracle. He was just your typical boy next door, who grew up in a very troubled family.

So what made Joseph great? Why does God devote more space in Genesis to his story than to any other individual? Because of Joseph's attitude, how he responded to difficult circumstances. That was the most remarkable thing about him.[8]

Attitude is fundamental to Joseph's story. In addition, when we search the Old Testament for foreshadowings of the coming Messiah, the one man who stands out is Joseph. The entire story of Joseph is a reminder to us of Jesus, who *"... came to that which was His own, but His own did not receive Him"* (John 1:11).

It will be helpful to look at the defining moments of Joseph's early life in the midst of a dysfunctional family. There are lessons in his experiences and his responses that may benefit contemporary believers:

I. THE DEFINING MOMENT OF BEING A FAVORITE:

We can assume that as Joseph goes through his many experiences, he learns that a person's greatest assets can also be their greatest hindrances.

---

8   Charles R. Swindoll, *Joseph: From Pit to Pinnacle, Bible Study Guide*
     (Fullerton, CA: Insight For Living, 1990), 75.

Joseph was favored, and it is good to be favored. However, to be a *favorite* implies that someone else is not, and that can be deadly.

Too often, parents overlook this fact. Parents may say, "I don't have a favorite, I just connect with that child more." However, that "connection" may be perceived as favoritism by the unconnected child. We parents must guard against unwittingly favoring one child over another in order that the seeds of discontent and unhappiness are not sown in our children.

When a child is a favorite amongst others, no matter how subtle the signs, that favoritism becomes a defining feature in the child's life. Being a favorite may ill-equip a child to deal with life's real challenges, while being the non-favorite so often leads to jealousy and a sense of resentment. Neither child enters life well prepared to live victoriously.

The issue of having been a favorite or a slightly disregarded child in the family can determine so much in people's lives. It can certainly effect future relationships. When crises occurs calling for maturity, such individuals will need a relationship with the Lord in order to remain well grounded. Joseph seems to have had that kind of relationship.

Somewhere in Joseph's childhood, he obviously established a relationship with God. This is one of those unrecorded facts that we know it happened as evidenced in his life. In fact, Joseph's relationship with God is about the only functional relationship that he has. This fact proves to be the key to his ability to withstand all that happens to him.

Did the favoritism that Jacob have for Joseph cause the dysfunction in their family? Certainly not, for favoritism cannot be the root cause of dysfunction. On the contrary, the dysfunction gave rise to the favoritism.

Quite frankly, Jacob should have known better. Jacob grew up in a home where he was his mother's favorite and his twin brother, Esau, was his father Isaac's favorite. The entire family was a mess. Now Jacob has his own family and things have not changed. His family is dysfunctional because he came out of dysfunction. The problem was never corrected, and Jacob perpetuates the problem perhaps in an even more pronounced way. Jacob's favorite son is Joseph, and this sets the tone for everything that will ensue. As a result of feeling excluded and disregarded, the brothers hate Joseph.

II. THE DEFINING MOMENT WHERE JOSEPH DISCOVERS THAT A FATHER'S FAVORITISM CAN PROVE FATAL FOR THE WHOLE FAMILY.

The brothers certainly exercised their own free will in what they did to Joseph, and it is certainly never right to blame bad behavior on heritage. Yet Jacob is not without fault in this matter. Maren Niehoff says, "... it is only the nature of Jacob's attitude to Joseph which creates the latter's peculiar position among the brothers." [9]

Why did the brothers hate Joseph so much? Before answering this question, let's reiterate what we have already stated in the Introduction, that these were not "good boys". These were mean men. Once again, Chuck Swindoll so brilliantly paints the scene of the home for us:

> The home in which Joseph was raised was comprised of a family filled with angry, jealous, and deceitful people. Then, within that hostile environment, for seventeen years, the other sons of Jacob had watched as their father played favorites with Joseph. Their jealousy had turned into resentment and hatred. Don't miss the closing statement in (Gen. 37:2–4). Joseph's brothers had come to despise their younger brother so severely that they could not even speak a kind word to him. Try to imagine the mounting pressure in that home. It was a giant powder keg on the verge of explosion. [10]

Having now observed the scenario, let us answer why the sons of Jacob hated Joseph so much:

Possibly Joseph was hated because of the godliness in his character. It is stated in Genesis 37:2 that Joseph returns with a bad report to his father about the behavior of the brothers. The nature of the report is not revealed, but the phrase *"a bad report"* or *"an evil report"* (in the King James version) may refer to something the brothers did that was outside God's will. These boys, whatever they did, must have done something seriously wrong. Speculation has been offered that since the phrase, *"... with his brothers,*

---

9   Maren Niehoff, *The Figure of Joseph in Post-Biblical Jewish Literature* (Netherlands: E.J. Brill, 1992), 84.

10   Charles R. Swindoll, *A Man of Integrity and Forgiveness: Joseph* (Nashville, TN: Word Publishing, 1998), 11.

the sons of Bilhah and the sons of Zilpah, his father's wives ..." (Genesis 37:2) is mentioned in the verse, it may have been something lascivious in nature. Such a claim cannot be substantiated, but it leaves one wondering. The other implication found in this verse is that the incident, whatever it was, may have been widely known in the family since so many names are mentioned. Jacob may have been the only one not aware of the infraction. Whatever it was, Joseph carried the report back to his father. He took it upon himself to see to it that his father was informed of the matter.

At a casual glance, it may appear that this was nothing more than Joseph being a tattletale, but do not be too hasty to make that judgement. It may be that he was currying favor by telling tales, but keep in mind that we do not know what the indiscretion was and we will never know. Perhaps it was something so horrendous that it needed to be told. Perhaps it was something that put someone's life in jeopardy. In that case, telling his father would have been a wise move on Joseph's part. We must be careful of judging Joseph's decision here since we do not know what the indiscretion was.

So, we have an introduction to a teenager of seventeen, and the first thing we learn of is his character; he is different from his brothers. It seems that at this early stage of his life, Joseph has already determined to take a stand for what is right in the eyes of God. Furthermore, over the next twenty years, one sad, pitiful event after another happens in his life, yet at no point does he waver from being faithful to God. Even while still a teenager, he is hated by his brothers for the godly character he exhibits.

Possibly, Joseph was hated because of his position. Fascinatingly, Genesis 37:3 says, *"Now Israel loved Joseph more than any of his other sons, because he had been born to him in his old age; and he made an ornate robe for him."* The New American Standard Version calls it "a varicolored tunic." In the King James version, it is referred to as a "coat of many colors." This was an ornate, multi-colored tunic or *ketonet passim* reaching down to the palms of the hands and down to the soles of his feet. It was a garment that was to cover the extremities and flow all the way down to the ground, and Jacob made this for Joseph – but did not make one for the other boys.

This raises another question: Why would Joseph need such a robe? This type of clothing is not what a man wore in the fields to work in those days. We know this because it is not the type of clothing worn for agricultural work in any part of the world. Never has been! It would have been too hot, too constricting and much too heavy. So why is this robe given such prominence in Scripture?

Jacob gave Joseph this robe because it was the garment of a supervisor, and essentially, in giving him this coat, he showed that he had no intention of letting Joseph work out in the fields alongside the others. His intention was for Joseph to oversee the other boys in the family, and the boys hated him because of that position.

But the story does not end there. That is not the only gift that Jacob bestows on Joseph. It is the one on which we always focus. There was also a parcel of land. In the New Testament, Jesus and His disciples are making their way through a particular region, and it said, *"So He came to a town in Samaria called Sychar, near the plot of ground Jacob had given to his son Joseph"* (John 4:5). Now, compare that with the only piece of ground that we know Jacob owned, which is found in Genesis 33, where it says, *"For a hundred pieces of silver, he [Jacob] bought from the sons of Hamor, the father of Shechem, the plot of ground where he pitched his tent"* (Genesis 33:19). As far as we know, that is the only property owned by Jacob, and somewhere between Genesis 33 and 37, Jacob gave that piece of ground to Joseph, and did not give any of it to the other brothers. We should keep in mind that Joseph was not the oldest, and giving this much to someone who is not the firstborn was contrary to the culture of the times. Therefore, it seems that Jacob truly intended for Joseph to rule over the family.

Perhaps in Jacob's old age, he saw what Potiphar and the jailer would later see in Joseph – leadership abilities. Joseph had management skills; he could organize people, manage and develop them. Jacob might have seen that, and he gave Joseph the only piece of land that he had and a supervisor's uniform to go with the land. Is it any wonder that these boys, who are possibly already disinclined to honor God's ways, would hate him? Genesis 37:4 tells us clearly: "When his brothers saw that their father loved him more than any of them, they hated him and could not speak a kind word to him."

All of this confirms that a father's favoritism can prove fatal for a family.

III. THE DEFINING MOMENT OF HOW GOD'S BLESSINGS CREATE JEALOUSY AMONG THE BRETHREN.

God forbid this should ever be the case in our lives, but it does happen. God does not intend it, but Satan draws up the blueprints for it.

You will recall that Joseph relates a dream to his brothers. This is a fascinating part of the story because nowhere is it stated that God told Joseph to tell the dream to his brothers. At seventeen, Joseph is immature and possibly displays elements of arrogance. This, however, changes as he matures.

In the familiar dream, the boys are in the field binding sheaves, and Joseph's sheaf stands erect while his brothers' sheaves bow down to his sheaf. Joseph tells this dream to his brothers. Many have speculated whether Joseph may have been somewhat of a braggart in those early years. This cannot be substantiated, but Joseph will be seen in later years saying something that does cause one to think that he is not quite ready for greatness and that a little seasoning might be in order. Joseph may also have been sincere, although a little naïve, not realizing the effect of telling such a dream to his brothers.

Whatever his motives, hatred mounts in his brothers, and no sooner does Joseph finish relating that dream than he starts describing another dream with similar results. Scripture implies that even his father, and possibly his mother, may have been getting a little tired of these dreams. Jacob starts to rebuke his favorite son in Genesis 37:10.

I have cited two reasons for the hatred of Joseph's brothers, and it is worth mentioning that Dr. Harold Willmington states that he believes there were three reasons why the boys were mad at Joseph:

Joseph had brought down upon him the wrath of his ten half-brothers. Three factors had led to his sad situation. 1) Because he had reported to his father some of the bad things the ten were doing (37:2). 2) Because he had become Jacob's favorite son. To show this special affection, the old man gave Joseph a long-sleeved brightly colored tunic (37:3). 3) Because of Joseph's strange dreams (a) in one of his dreams they were all in the field binding sheaves, when suddenly his sheaf stooped up and their sheaves all gathered around it and bowed low before it. (b) During his second dream he saw the sun, moon, and eleven stars bow low before him (37:9).[11]

Do not let it be lost on you that the intent of the brothers was to kill Joseph, according to Genesis 37:18. Jacob sends Joseph out to check on the welfare of his brothers as they watch their herds in Shechem. A stranger tells him that his brothers have left Shechem and directs Joseph to Dothan. It is there, as they see him approaching, that the brothers formulate a plot to murder "this dreamer", Joseph. Had not Reuben and Judah stepped in to plead for a softer treatment, they might have murdered Joseph then and there. Instead, they strip him of his tunic and put him in a pit until they can devise a plan for what to do with him next.

Experiences like the one that happened to Joseph are hard to comprehend because it is not often in modern Western civilization (or any other culture around the world) that these things occur among siblings, or at least not to this degree. Yet cast into a pit and left to die is where the eventual patriarch of the Hebrew people now finds himself. It is indeed Joseph's defining moment of realization; he is forced to know at last the full extent of his brothers' jealousy.

I think if I were Joseph, I might have said to myself, "So much for dreaming. So much for being a supervisor. So much for greatness. If I ever get out of here, I'm *done* with this dreaming. All it ever got me was time in the pit. I know God is with me and I know that the blessings of the heavenly Father are upon me, but to have those blessings at the price of being almost murdered by ten lousy, jealous brothers? No more of this, Lord."

---

11   H.L. Willmington, *Willmington's Guide to the Bible, Vol. 1, Old Testament* (Wheaton, IL: Tyndale House Publishers, 1986), 53-54.

IV. THE DEFINING MOMENT OF LEARNING FROM EXPERIENCE.

Joseph is learning lessons at this point and until they are fully learned, he will not be able to properly deal with or embrace his brothers. Every step along the way reveals that Joseph has learned a little more. He learns lessons in Dothan about holding his peace, but perhaps he has not learned quite as much as he will have learned by the time he sees his brothers again years later in Egypt. Joseph is extremely blessed of God, but the whole situation at this point is reminiscent of a celebrity or a professional athlete who cannot handle success. Joseph still has some growing up to do, as Sidney Greidanus points out. Right after relating the first dream, Joseph does not seem to "get it" that the family does not want to hear his dreams.

> Joseph is further characterized by the dialogue: his insistence on telling his dreams that his brothers and even his father and mother bow down to him. The young Joseph is sketched as immature, unwise, boastful, and extremely talkative. This changes drastically when Joseph meets up with his brothers in Dothan. Here Joseph is passive and says not a single word.[12]

Greidanus is correct about Joseph not speaking another word, or at least if he did, it was not recorded. In fact, although more of the story is related about him, Joseph is not heard speaking again until he is talking to Potiphar's wife in Egypt.

As alluded to earlier, had it not been for Reuben and Judah, Joseph would have been dead, but that does not mean that Reuben and Judah are innocent. Each had their own motive for keeping Joseph alive. Reuben was hoping to return him to his father and so escape censure, and Judah wanted to sell him to make a profit. Interestingly, it is from the tribe of Judah that the Savior, Jesus Christ, comes. Jesus is sold and put to death by His own people, and here Joseph is sold and almost put to death by his own people. The following chapter of Genesis also spells out in great detail the evil that was in Judah's heart and life, and it further evokes the displeasure of God.

---

12   Sidney Greidanus, *Preaching Christ from Genesis: Foundations for Expository Sermons* (Grand Rapids, MI: Eerdmans Publishing Co., 2007), 338.

It is amazing to me that in everything that Joseph goes through, we hear no mention of protesting. We are not told, at this point, that he called out. Later in Genesis, the brothers recall that they did indeed hear him call; a memory seemingly dislodged only by their own troubles. Yet the lack of its mention at this point in the story suggests that Joseph may be learning what we are told in Proverbs, that "the prudent hold their tongue" (Proverbs 10:19). Perhaps, too, Joseph is beginning to recognize that God is working in the midst of his trials.

Whatever else Joseph is learning at this point remains a mystery, but he has seen, and will see in years to come, much misfortune, anger, jealousy, hatred, rejection, slavery, attempted murder, and a host of other examples of man's inhumanity to man. We are also not told how Joseph processes these experiences, but he obviously handles them in a way that grooms him into the political and national hero that he later becomes. None of this is known to Joseph or his brothers yet. We can conclude from his eventual maturity that Joseph learns a lot during his early years; lessons about handling family dysfunction, the correct way to handle his own position as favorite, and how to deal with his father's personal shortcomings.

V. THE DEFINING MOMENTS FOR THE BELIEVER'S LEARNING.

When so much space is given in Scripture to a story like this, it is obviously intended to do more than relate events; it also imparts lessons for the believer. Clearly, favoritism and neglect can be deadly. Never has there been, and never will there be, a generation that does not need to heed the warning signs.

For the sake of illustration, let's consider the 1984 movie *Amadeus*. So much of what was portrayed on screen was largely fictionalized by Hollywood, but the plot certainly brings into sharper relief some of our study's focus. The movie tells the story of the relationship between Wolfgang Amadeus Mozart and Antonio Salieri. Antonia Salieri was a brilliant musician, court composer for the Holy Roman Emperor and Austrian imperial Kapellmeister from 1788 to 1824, at a time when opera was coming into its own. Wolfgang Amadeus Mozart was an even more brilliant composer; a genius and recognized as such by all who met him. The movie portrays Salieri as having a raging jealousy of Mozart.

On the screen, Salieri tries to bargain with God, asking God to make him a great composer. He sees the rise of Mozart and says, "Lord, let me celebrate your glory through music and be celebrated myself." It was not so much that he wanted to celebrate God, but that he wanted to be celebrated himself. He goes on to plead with God, "Make me famous throughout the world. Make me immortal. After I die, let people speak my name forever with love for what I have written. In return, I will give you my chastity, my industry, my deepest humility in every area of my life."

Yet such fame eludes Salieri while there is a meteoric rise for Mozart. He becomes popular with the emperor, and all the crown heads of Europe are fascinated with his music. As a result, Salieri throws his faith away as he says to God, "You and I are enemies now. I will do everything I can to destroy the gift that You put in Mozart." And that is how he spends his last years. Salieri, a wonderful musician and composer, was so jealous and envious of Mozart that he could not see what God was doing in his own life through his teaching of students like Franz Liszt, Franz Schubert and Ludwig Van Beethoven. The fable concludes that because of his insane jealousy of Mozart, Salieri could not see how God was using him to raise up a new generation of the greatest classical composers that ever lived.[13]

How much of that story is true is widely debated, but it portrays the truth that jealousy can be deadly – if not physically, then certainly emotionally, psychologically, and spiritually. When you and I, as children of the living God, are jealous of the gift that God puts in a brother or sister's life, that jealousy puts a film over our spiritual eyes, a wax in our spiritual ears, and it will petrify and ossify our spiritual heart so that we no longer see, hear, or feel God at all.

---

13   *Amadeus,* directed by Miloš Forman, Orion Pictures, 1984, summarization.

In this chapter, I used the movie *Amadeus* as an illustration of jealousy's destructive power, and I want to relate a contrasting true story of someone who did *not* allow jealousy to destroy him. F.B. Meyer was a nineteenth century preacher in London. To the one side of the church where he pastored was the beloved G. Campbell Morgan, preaching at Westminster Chapel. To the other side of Meyer's church was the prince of preachers, Charles Haddon Spurgeon, preaching at the Metropolitan Tabernacle. Joseph Parker, another great London preacher was also nearby preaching at the great City Temple Church.

Pastoring in the shadow of these great preachers, Meyer could stand on the steps of his own church and in the distance see the thousands flocking to the Tabernacle and the Chapel. He could see the royal carriages going by, the aristocracy and the upper-crust of England going to hear Spurgeon, Morgan, and Parker. Richard Phillips is one among many authors who describe the details:

> The gifted preacher F.B. Meyer struggled with envy. God called him to serve in London at the same time as Charles Haddon Spurgeon, arguably the greatest preacher who ever lived. So, despite his ability and hard work, Meyer would stand outside his church and watch the carriages flow by to Spurgeon's Metropolitan Tabernacle. Later in life, it happened again, as G. Campbell Morgan eclipsed Meyer's success. When they spoke together at conferences, vast crowds listened to Morgan, then left when Meyer was to preach.
>
> Convicted over his bitter spirit, Meyer committed himself to pray for Morgan, reasoning that the Holy Spirit would not allow him to envy a man for whom he prayed. He was right. God enabled Meyer to rejoice in Morgan's preaching. People heard him saying: "Have you heard Campbell Morgan preach? Did you hear that message this morning? My, God is upon that man!" In response to Meyer's prayers, Morgan's church so overflowed that people came and filled Meyer's church, too.[14]

---

14   Richard D. Phillips, *The Masculine Mandate: God's Calling to Men* (Lake Mary, FL: Reformation Trust Publishing, 2010), 148.

Speaking about this situation in Meyer's life and the temptation to jealousy that can rear its ugly head for anyone, R.T. Kendall, who later pastored where G. Campbell Morgan pastored, expounds on Meyer's words:

> Meyer said to some friends, "It was easy to pray for the success of Morgan when he was in America. But when he came to England and to a church near mine, it was something different. The old Adam in me was inclined to jealousy, but I got my heel upon his head, and whether I felt right toward my friend, I determined to act right."[15]

These stories are very well documented about Meyer. Further insight regarding relations between these great nineteenth century preachers is given by Warren Wiersbe:

> Meyer said, "I find in my own ministry that supposing I pray for my own little flock, 'God bless me, God fill my pews, God send me a revival,' I miss the blessing; but as I pray for my big brother, Mr. Spurgeon, on the right-hand side of my church, 'God bless him'; or my other big brother, Campbell Morgan, on the other side of my church, 'God bless him'; I am sure to get a blessing without praying for it, for the overflow of their cups fills my little bucket."[16]

Finally, the best statement made regarding the jealousy that Meyer experienced and repented of was related by Charles Ray in 1905 when, after Spurgeon died, Meyer was called on to say something about Spurgeon at his funeral. Ray quotes Meyer as saying:

> "You may well print the Jubilee number of Mr. Spurgeon's sermons in gold! Gold befits gold," says the Rev. F.B. Meyer. "I can never tell my indebtedness to them. As I read them week by week in my young manhood, they gave me a grip of the Gospel that I can never lose, and gave an ideal of its presentation in nervous, transparent and forcible language which has colored my entire ministry. It is marvelous to notice, also, that the last volume, just published, seems to lack nothing in comparison with those that have gone

---

15   R.T. Kendall, *Jealousy: The Sin No One Talks About* (Lake Mary, FL: Charisma House, 2010), 24.

16   Warren W. Wiersbe and Lloyd Merle Perry, *The Wycliffe Handbook of Preaching and Preachers* (Chicago, IL: Moody Press, 1984), 193.

before. What a blessed ministry his has been to myriads!"[17]

In light of Meyer's words, one would have to wonder what Spurgeon himself thought of Meyer. Spurgeon's exact words were, "Meyer preaches as a man who has seen God face to face."[18]

Now, I ask you this as I ask it of my own heart: Where is that spirit today? Where is it, not only among pastors, but among brothers and sisters in the Lord, and brothers and sisters born of the same parents? Where is that among husbands and wives? Do our children see it demonstrated? Where are the kind words for one another? Where is the genuine pleasure in what God does for and in another? We have grown so jealous of one another and we think so highly of our own attainments that when someone does well, we often say, "I suspect something deceptive is going on there!"

My dear friends who read these words, I call on every child of God to heed this warning: God may withhold his blessing in the future unless we curb our jealousy. Others might have been as face to face with God as we have, or maybe even more. We as God's people – of all people – need to recognize the gift that God has placed in someone else and not be given to jealousy, but seek to lift the hearts of others. Be grateful that God's Kingdom is advanced!

Jealousy rips up lives, homes, families, businesses, governments, and yes, even churches. Jealousy exists where there is a lack of passion for God. Anytime a person experiences jealousy, it is because his or her heart lacks godly passion.

Joseph's brothers had no passion for God whatsoever, and they saw that Joseph did, plain and simple. They saw it in Joseph's character, in his nature, and in his stand for God, but that same passion was not evident in their own lives. They hated him. And the reason for their hatred was their own lack of passion for the Lord.

---

17   Charles Ray, *A Marvelous Ministry: The Story of C.H. Spurgeon's Sermons, 1855-1905* (London: Passmore and Alabaster, 1905), 119.

18   David Allen, "Preaching, Part 4: Learning from the History of Preaching," Theological Matters: Insights from Southwestern, Southwestern Baptist Theological Seminary, entry posted October 20, 2011, http://www.theologicalmatters.com/index. php/2011/10/20/preaching-part-4/ [accessed September 1, 2012].

What is the lesson we should learn from all of this? Fall in love with Jesus so intently, and there will not be any complaining about what someone else has. In fact, there may be some excitement for them. When you and I have a genuine passion for God, we cannot help but rejoice when the brethren show evidence of God's work in their lives.

How do we obtain that passion? A good place to start is to get close to that brother or sister by supporting them in prayer, as F.B. Meyer did. Follow Meyer's example. Try praying for that brother or sister in the Lord. Pray that they will be so blessed that there will not be room enough for them to receive the blessing – and then just hang around! Be close by so that some of the overflow washes over you, and you begin to know yourself cleansed, restored and forgiven.

CHAPTER TWO

JOSEPH'S DEFINING MOMENTS IN A DEMORALIZING FIX

Fights are bad enough, but when families fight, it is an awful thing. Those struggles are usually far more vindictive than when strangers argue. Family feuds can be incredibly ugly. This is the reason that when disagreements split a church, the pain reaches deeper than so many other hurts; Christians see each other as family.

In Genesis 37 there is an ongoing family feud. There are ten brothers, not counting the youngest (Benjamin), who hate and despise one brother in the family – Joseph. They hate him because of his character, position, dreams, robe, and probably for a parcel of land that was given him. You name it, they have it against him, or so it would seem. When a person is already hated, an unregenerate person will easily find more reasons hate him. The brothers were not wise enough to discern that they hated Joseph because of the hand of God on his life. They were out of God's will. He was in God's will, and they could not stand him for that position. Having God's *favor* is not necessarily the same thing as being a *favorite.* Having God's favor is a good thing. Being Jacob's favorite in that family nearly caused a fatality.

The brothers' hatred for Joseph was unwarranted, for Joseph had done nothing serious enough to provoke this hate. He may have been immature in telling them his dreams, but he was naïve, not malicious. It was an unprovoked hatred, and this was partially Jacob's fault. He had put his sons into situations that would breed hatred for their brother. We fathers need to remember that favoritism (among many other things) is exasperating to our children, and it is our responsibility to avoid this (Ephesians 6:4). Below the surface, the brothers despised what their father was doing, or neglecting to do. As a result, they refused to be reconciled to Joseph, and eventually they attempted to kill him.

When a family has that much disruption, hatred and bitterness, something is bound to explode. Before swords are drawn, rights are claimed, and scores are settled, we should notice that we have more than one cheek. When the sting on one cheek is felt, it is often too difficult and painful to consider offering the other one, and yet, as David Augsburger writes, that is exactly what we should do.

> If you intend to claim all your rights in life, to even all scores against you, to demand every penny ever owed you, then go ahead.

> But if you give no inch, expect no second chances; if you show no mercy, do not hope for mercy; if you extend no forgiveness you can expect none. Life, love, mercy and forgiveness are all two-way streets. To receive, you must give humbly, aware that you are constantly in need of the understanding and acceptance of others and loving mercy of God.

> "All they that take the sword shall perish by the sword," said Jesus Christ. Is there any doubt? [19]

CONFRONTATION ENSUES

The action starts when Jacob's sons are working the pasture, tending to their father's flock in Shechem, and Jacob sends Joseph to check on them. Do not be mistaken; Jacob loved all his sons. Joseph may have been a favorite, but we see evidence here that Jacob loved all his boys and was concerned about their welfare.

Jacob had good reason to be concerned. Shechem, the place, was named after Shechem, the man. Sometime earlier, Shechem had raped Jacob's daughter Dinah. In revenge, Simeon and Levi had slaughtered every man in Shechem. The brothers are now back in Shechem, and obviously, Jacob is concerned that there might be some residual anger about this whole ordeal.

Joseph arrives in Shechem, and Genesis 37:15 tells us, *"a man found him wandering around in the fields and asked him, 'What are you looking for?'"*

---

19   David Augsburger, *70 x 7: The Freedom of Forgiveness*
     (Chicago, IL: Moody Press, 1970), 121.

Here is a nameless, faceless man. Why is he mentioned? Note him, for he forms an important element in the story, as we shall see later.

Joseph explains that he is looking for his brothers, and the man tells him that they have gone to Dothan. The names of the places mentioned so far have an interesting symbolism: The brothers had been raised in Hebron, which means, "place of alliance," or "place of fellowship." It could mean, "the place where you come together." They go to Shechem on the slopes of Mount Ebel. Mount Ebel means "shoulder." It conveys an idea of strength or power.

They leave the place of unity and moral strength, Hebron, and they leave the other place of strength, Shechem. Their physical leaving seems to mirror a moral "leaving" which is already in motion: It is in Hebron that Reuben, the oldest, commits incest with his father's concubine and in the very next chapter we see that Judah, too, leaves this place of strength or purity; he commits incest with his daughter-in-law. It is true that he does not know she is his daughter-in-law; he thinks she is a prostitute, but that does not make it any more right. Sleeping with a prostitute has never been acceptable in God's eyes. We see clearly that Reuben and Judah have left the place of moral strength along with Simeon and Levi, who murdered all the men in Shechem.

Where do the brothers go? They go to Dothan, which means "two cities," "two cisterns," or "two feasts". Dothan is the place of the material, the tangible, and the physical. There is something about the sequence of Hebron, then Shechem, and then Dothan that seems to pull them away from the place of fellowship, strength, and blessing, to a place where they are out of God's will.

In Dothan, they see Joseph approaching. He is wearing the elaborate garment his father gave him, his *ketonet passim*. Nahum Sarna paints a picture of this garment for us.

> Its precise nature eludes us, it being variously but uncertainly explained as "a coat of many colors," "a long-sleeved robe," "ornamented tunic"; there is no doubt, however, that it was a token of special favor and perhaps, too, of luxury and lordship, of

superiority and supervisory over his brothers. In a later age it was the distinctive dress of the virgin daughters of royalty. At any rate, to the brothers the coat was a hated symbol of favoritism and a cause of discord.[20]

As Joseph approaches, that royal robe shines in the sunlight, and he becomes a walking, neon billboard of his father's favoritism.

How did the brothers know it was Joseph approaching? Well, the boys were not color blind. They could tell it was him by the colors of the flowing robe. As he walks closer, they hatch their plan. "Here comes this dreamer," they say. "Let's kill him!" (paraphrase).

We see in this story how various plans turn sour:

Jacob's plan for Joseph to check on his other sons turns into a nightmare. They decide to kill him, then soften it somewhat by stripping him of his robe, throwing him into a pit and selling him.

A word about that pit: Years ago, I lived on a seven-acre farm in rural Kentucky which had a sixteen-thousand gallon cistern for gathering rain water that was used for drinking and household use. The water ran off the roof, into gutters covered with screens to keep debris out, and into the cistern. From there, it flowed via underground pipes into two hot and cold water storage tanks in the basement of the house. There it went through a filtration system for purification before being used. That was our only water. During times of drought when the water level dipped below the pump, we had to pay to have the fire department come out and deliver water to fill the cistern.

Having lived where cisterns are still in use, I know full well what they are for, how they are maintained, and what they look like. It is likely that this pit or cistern in Genesis could have held between sixteen thousand and twenty thousand gallons of rain water. If a person fell into one of these holding tanks, whether half full or dry, they could well die in there. Imagine the fear if no help arrived – of having to sleep and starve in that pit. Think about what would happen if no one came for days or weeks. If it rained and

---

20   Nahum M. Sarna, *Understanding Genesis: The Heritage of Biblical Israel* (New York, NY: McGraw-Hill Book Company, 1966), 212.

the pit started to fill up, one might float a little higher up, but that would take a long time, and if the water rose only half way to the top, one might not be able to reach up and clamber out. A person might well drown there.

We are not told what Joseph's response is; whether he screams, cries or fights back. Later in the book of Genesis the brothers do recall *"how distressed he was when he pleaded with us for his life ..."* (Genesis 42:21), but the details and the intensity of his response are not recorded. Clearly, his father's plan had gone awry; what Joseph thought was a fact-finding mission to go and check on his brothers had turned into an apparent nightmare.

For the brothers' part, their plan turns into a nightmare, too. They hoped that by disposing of Joseph they would win more affection from their father, but Jacob's response belies this hope. Their plan avails them little.

It is becoming obvious that despite being the oldest, Reuben never leads this family because he lacks integrity. It is Judah who ends up leading the clan, despite his own downfalls. Judah suggests the idea of selling Joseph into slavery, which they do. The brothers then agree to dip Joseph's coat in the blood of a slaughtered goat and return it to Jacob, claiming that he has been killed by a wild beast. We are told in verse 32, *"They took the ornate robe back to their father and said, 'We found this. Examine it to see whether it is your son's robe'"* (Genesis 37:32).

Do you notice something in that remark? It is obvious that the brothers feel anger, disdain, and resentment toward Joseph, for they say "your son's" and not "our brother's" tunic. Their words imply, "We are not your sons. The only son you have is Joseph, and he is not our brother." These boys are bitter, indeed.

As the saying goes, "What goes around comes around." Deception, which played such a part in Jacob's own early adulthood, is coming back to haunt him. Surely the boys are thinking, "Joseph is gone, and now Dad will love us." As it turns out, the boys do not even have to tell the lie about Joseph's fate to their father because Jacob offers the apparent conclusion in verse 33, when he says, *"It is my son's robe! Some ferocious animal has devoured him. Joseph has surely been torn to pieces"* (Genesis 37:33).

In my imagination, I see the boys as they wipe the sweat from their brows and whisper, "Whew! He bought it!" They never say what happened. They planned to tell a lie about Joseph having been devoured, but when they finally give their father the tunic, they let him draw his own conclusion. That, by the way, is bearing false witness. One can bear false witness without saying a word.

This is where the plan backfires on the boys: Jacob's spirit is so crushed that he vows he will never get over it and will carry his sorrow to his grave. They thought he would love them more, but Jacob is unable to love in his extreme unhappiness. The boys' plan has turned into a nightmare.

For Joseph, however, his nightmare is turned into a plan! What appears to be the end of the line is actually a silver lining, although it will take time for God's full plan to be revealed.

In verse 27, we are told the boys decide to sell Joseph to the Ishmaelites, who are descendants of Ishmael, the illegitimate son of Abraham and Hagar. They are cousins of the Hebrews, in a sense. It is, however, rather puzzling why he is *not* sold to the Ishmaelites. That was the plan. Instead, we are told in verse 28 that the Midianite traders arrived. It is highly possible that the boys sold him to the Midianites, and the Midianites later sold him to the Ishmaelites. The Midianites are closely related to the Ishmaelites, for Midian was the son of Abraham and Katoura, Abraham's second wife after Sarah died.

Thus it appears that Joseph may have been sold as many as three times to various middlemen; first to the Midianites, who sold him to the Ishmaelites, who then sold him to the Egyptians. A possible fourth sale may have occurred on the auction block in Egypt, where Potiphar bought him.

Here is the point: Joseph leaves his father's house in order to find his brothers who are lost. Along the way, he finds a nameless, faceless person who hears the brothers' conversations and knows of their movements. Joseph goes to his own, and his own receive him not. They strip him of his robe and sell him for twenty pieces of silver. There is hardly a more complete picture in the Old Testament of the Messiah.

Jesus left the Father's house, and came looking for His own. The Holy Spirit listens to every conversation and gives directions; Jesus stays in tune with the Holy Spirit and with the heavenly Father throughout His earthly life. When Jesus finds His own, they despise and reject Him. They strip Him of His garments and sell Him for thirty pieces of silver (Matthew 26:15). Joseph does not know it yet, but his nightmare both foreshadows Christ's coming and forms part of a plan for the salvation of the Hebrew people.

IN THE MEANTIME, WHAT JOSEPH IS LEARNING

Joseph is learning lessons from dealing with his brothers. Both Joseph and his brothers eventually learn that what goes around, comes around, and often in greater measure than what was given out in the first place. Right now, Joseph does not understand this, but the providence of God is something that becomes more and more evident as the story progresses.

Think about that long, arduous, and lonely trip to Egypt when God must have seemed strangely quiet. Joseph may have ridden, but he may well have been chained and made to walk all the way. How he must have thought, "God, you are allowing me to go into a land where you are not! How can that be? God, this was not part of the plan. This was not in the dream. God, I'm frightened. I don't know where they are taking me. God, let me go home. Why are you silent, God?" Yes, Joseph is learning about the silence of God during a waiting period.

I have often wondered, in the silent moments of life when God is the quietest, could it be those are the moments when God is the kindest? When God is strangely quiet, it seems we miss Him and reflect on Him all the more. God's silence can often be deafening.

What will also be evident is that Joseph is in the process of dignifying the trial. In the New Testament, James says, *"Consider it pure joy, my brothers and sisters, whenever you face trials of many kinds, because you know that the testing of your faith produces perseverance"* (James 1:2–3). Obviously, Joseph is not familiar with that Bible verse, but he demonstrates that he knows the principle, a principle that R.T. Kendall discusses:

We therefore are to consider having to face trials of many kinds as pure joy. It is thus a word often used in an ironic sense. What would naturally make us feel the opposite – to be upset or feel sorry for ourselves – is to be taken as a wonderful privilege, or opportunity, instead.

Who enjoys the feeling of disgrace? It would, after all, be abnormal to enjoy this. Unless, that is, one had a definite reason for feeling this way. Moses did. He considered disgrace as more valuable than earthly luxury – all because it put him in good stead for the future. Jesus endured the cross because of the joy set before Him (Heb. 12:2). Joseph, the same.[21]

Genesis 37:36 tells us that Joseph is sold to the Egyptian Pharaoh's officer, the captain of the bodyguard. Interestingly, Pharaoh's name is never revealed, although Potiphar's is. Why does the Holy Spirit not give us the name of the more eminent person, the Pharaoh? I wonder if it is because of another lesson that Joseph is learning; that what impresses man does not always impress God. It is almost as if God is saying, "I have prepared Potiphar and his home for you, and that is all you need to know for now."

F.B. Meyer beautifully alludes to what may have been God's strategy in this traumatic event, and how He continues to work with those of us who are His children:

> It was the work of a few minutes; and then Joseph found himself one of a long line of fettered slaves, bound for a foreign land. Was not this almost worse than death? What anguish still rent his young heart! How eager his desire to send just one last message to his father! And with all these thoughts, there would mingle a wondering thought of the great God whom he had learned to worship. What would He say to this? Little did he think then that hereafter he should look back on that day as one of the most gracious links in a chain of loving providences; or that he should ever say, "Be not grieved, nor angry with yourselves: God did send me here before you." It is very sweet, as life passes by, to be able to look back on

---

21   R.T. Kendall, *Pure Joy* (London: Hodder & Stoughton, 2004), 13.

dark and mysterious events, and to trace the hand of God where we once saw only the malice and cruelty of man. And no doubt the day is coming when we shall be able to speak thus of all the dark passages of our life.[22]

God was in control of the circumstances of Joseph's experience. This does not, however, imply that God caused the bad things to happen. Rather, God's scepter was swinging over the affairs of men, and His providential hand was leading in Joseph's life. Each event and lesson learned led to the next defining moment, all culminating in Joseph's eventual forgiveness and his full embracing of that forgiveness.

There are many lessons in Joseph's story that you and I as contemporary believers in Christ can learn from, but for now let us focus on two major conclusions that can be drawn from the story so far:

I. WHEN WE ARE OUTSIDE OF GOD'S WILL, PLANS AND DREAMS BECOME NIGHTMARES.

It is a dangerous thing for us to be away from the place of blessing. That is why the Psalmist reminds the child of God, *"Whoever dwells in the shelter of the Most High will rest in the shadow of the Almighty"* (Psalm 91:1).

The principle that I spoke of earlier, that what "goes around comes around" applies negatively when a person is outside of God's will. As Christians, we so often walk into what we have convinced ourselves is the will of God, only to discover later that our personal dreams and plans are not in His will. Pain and difficulties for ourselves and others are usually the result.

A by-product of being outside the will of God is frustration. This leads to all sorts of dysfunctional states of mind such as anger, distraction, impulsive behavior, a bitter spirit, etc., and often metastasizes into advanced stages of disrupted harmony in relationships. When you and I are outside of God's will, our plan and dreams can indeed become nightmares.

---

22   F.B. Meyer, *Joseph: Beloved, Hated, Exalted* (New York, NY: Fleming H. Revell Company, reprint 1911), 124.

II. WHEN WE ARE IN GOD'S WILL, NIGHTMARES MAY CONCEAL GOD'S PLANS.

How is it that things similar to what happened to Joseph happen to the child of God? When a Christian is in God's will, why do bad things still happen? This would take centuries to answer, and yet centuries have come and gone and mankind still has not fully understood this phenomenon. We know, however, that bad things can and frequently do happen to people who are in God's will.

Often we Christians go through unbelievable difficulties, darkness, struggles, traumas, and perplexities, and we wonder why God is so quiet. Sometimes the quietness during these difficult times may simply be to keep God's plans hidden for a time, to be revealed at a later time. Often we can look back and see in the "rearview mirror" how God moved.

Have you noticed that if nothing bad ever happened in life – if everything was good all of the time – how difficult it would be to look back and trace the hand of God? We go through times where we cannot figure out how we could possibly emerge victorious from the ordeal, but at the finish line, so often we look back and see God's hand over it all. Seeing how God worked after we have passed through the hard times leaves us with an illustration of how He may provide for us in the future. One thing I know: God's providential care will be illuminated at some point in all our lives. In the meantime, it may be that God's perfect will and plan remain concealed for a time.

LEARNING TO EMBRACE FORGIVENESS

In chapters one and two of this study, some defining moments in Joseph's life have been discussed. The story started in Genesis, chapter 37, and it does not take long before the action is in full swing, as Solomon Goldman points out.

> We have barely read a dozen verses and already we sense the tenseness of the situation and surmise the stirring happenings that lie ahead. Our curiosity is aroused, imagination keyed up, attention riveted, and eyes glued on Joseph. We follow him eagerly,

breathlessly, up to that momentous climax when he makes himself known to his brothers. Who of us, asked Tolstoy, has not wept over this story?[23]

I, for one, have wept over this story more in the last few years than at any other time in my life. Little by little, God the Father reveals things that Joseph needs to learn. When we immerse ourselves in the story, we continue to learn of God's forgiveness. To this day, I never read about Joseph without eagerly anticipating some new thing that God will reveal to me.

We are at that point in the story now, where, along with Joseph, we are about to enter Egypt and learn many new things. I am not talking about new truth, but about new aspects of old truths that lead us, the reader, into a stronger faith and a closer walk with our Lord.

The story contains much that you and I may think we already know. Some of us have known these stories since our childhood; they are as familiar to us as are the old, dark, basement Sunday school classrooms where we learned them. Aren't we growing too old for them? Far from it. I am convinced that the more we read and absorb of Joseph's story – and all the others of Scripture – the deeper the truths God reveals to us, and the more we find in them to apply to our own situations.

Let us travel on to the next stage in the journey: Egypt and the auction block. But do not tarry long. Dinner is served at Potiphar's house, and troubles loom on the horizon. How will Joseph handle them all? Surely this is way too much for one young man to endure?

---

23   Solomon Goldman, *The Book of Human Destiny, Vol. 2: In The Beginning* (New York, NY: Harper & Brothers Publishers, 1949), 108.

CHAPTER THREE

JOSEPH'S DEFINING MOMENTS IN
ANOTHER DOMESTIC FIASCO

If Joseph thought he had learned enough about family dysfunction, he was sorely mistaken. He was getting ready to learn about it from another angle and with different dynamics. Had Joseph ever encountered sexual temptation prior to entering Egypt? Obviously, he had witnessed the horrible consequences of such sin in the lives of his brothers, but Scripture does not bear out that Joseph himself had ever been tempted in this way. That, however, is about to change.

Little is also known about Joseph's journey to Egypt. From previous chapters, it is known that Joseph is possibly sold many times prior to his entrance into Potiphar's house. He is auctioned off like an Angus bull, purchased by Pharaoh and delivered to Potiphar.

The fascinating aspect of all this is how Joseph comes through such adversity, and yet he is described as a successful and prosperous man. Somehow Joseph overcomes all his trauma, gaining the victory over loneliness, mistreatment and abuse. Incidentally, he remains single until he is somewhere near the age of thirty-seven or thirty-eight.

Once again, this chapter will also not deal with forgiveness. That is yet to come as events unfold. In the meantime, temptation, the subject of this chapter, must be faced and dealt with as part of the process that eventually leads to forgiveness.

With all that Joseph experiences, a sense of entitlement could so easily have become a part of his thinking to ease the pain his brothers caused. This never happens with Joseph.

In addition to loneliness and adverse circumstances, Joseph now begins to experience the temptation to be immoral. Until we, too, have emerged from the kinds of character-building trials he faced, we may not be ready to receive a passing grade in the arena of sexual temptation as

Joseph did. People often make the statement, "God will not give you more than you can handle." I always want to ask, "Where do you find that in Scripture?" Actually, I find that to be an untrue statement. God often allows us to have more than we can handle, proving that we need to rely on His sufficiency. Quite frequently, I encounter things I cannot handle, but when I completely turn it over the Lord, I discover God is sufficient to handle it for me. We should, however, remember that Scripture teaches us that God never allows a child of God to be *tempted* beyond what he or she is able to handle (1 Cor. 10:13).

How did Joseph attain his eventual success in the face of all he went through? How could he become prosperous with such a beginning? Very simply; he made a resolute determination to follow God *no matter what.* When everything else fell apart in his life, it was his determination to remain true to God that saw him succeed in the end.

Joseph is now sold to an officer of Pharaoh. This man was captain of the bodyguard, according to Genesis 39:1, and Pharaoh's chief executioner. His position may have been similar to that of a cabinet member of the President of the United States. He was comparable to the head of the FBI or the Secret Service or maybe the Director of Homeland Security. Potiphar's position was to discover plots against Pharaoh and to diffuse them, then to see that the people who were responsible for those plots were "taken care of." This was a great office with tremendous responsibility, and God saw to it that Joseph was deposited right there in order to "set up shop," so to speak, in that household.

Another thing we should keep in mind is that the odds were stacked against Joseph's survival. He is a young teenager who is going to be a slave. He has no idea what lies ahead. He has to learn a new language. He is a Hebrew in a Gentile world, a young person in an adult world, and a single man in a married world. Living a life of mediocrity and resigning from following God would have been a very easy thing to do. Yet regardless of the odds, Joseph does not do this. It is an astounding fact that Joseph had such maturity at this early stage of life. Possibly it was developed in his father's dysfunctional household. He certainly needed that maturity because he is now entering another, an even greater dysfunctional household.

JOSEPH'S EXPERIENCES IN ANOTHER DYSFUNCTIONAL HOUSEHOLD.

Genesis 39 documents very well that Joseph found favor in Potiphar's sight, so much so that Potiphar made Joseph overseer of everything he owned. It is not known what Potiphar gave Joseph to do at the start. Perhaps it was something menial, but Potiphar obviously observed that Joseph was capable, bright, articulate, ambitious, and no doubt served Potiphar very well. It is likely that Joseph had an excellent attitude. He consistently put his hand to the plow and did the work as required in spite of being single, lonely, frightened, hurt, and perhaps inwardly bitter about what his brothers had done to him.

For the way he worked, Potiphar puts Joseph in charge of the entire household. Now, what if Joseph had worked while, in the words of contemporary culture, "packing an attitude?" What if he had shown up each day with cynicism, anger and bitterness? What if he had said, "That's too menial. I wore a coat of many colors in my country. I wore a supervisor's uniform, and you want me to do what?" Regardless of the standing he is assigned in this new culture, Joseph consistently exhibits the attitude of, "I'm going to do my best in this situation." Attitudes certainly affect everything we do in life, and they can make or break us.

Attitudes affect our relationships, in particular. In fact they do more than affect them, they define them. Great attitudes help us build relationships with the people we work with, live with and interact with on a daily basis. I have noticed, for instance, that the people I had pastored over the years often remember very little about the sermons I had preached, and yet keenly remember how I had interacted with them. Attitudes shape our relationships and define how people remember us. In addition, our attitudes have a lot to do with people's willingness to forgive us when we are wrong in certain circumstances.

Joseph never displays an attitude of, "No, I won't do this. Not gonna hang my hat on that rack. Too much baggage and too much upset. Too much toxicity and drama for my life." We see none of this in his spirit. In fact, about the only tool that Joseph can hold onto, embrace and use is his attitude. That is where his rise to success starts. More than anything else, it is the excellent attitude he cultivates from the start that affects what will happen to him twenty years down the road in life. That is a long time to have a good attitude, but Joseph committed himself to it and reaps its inevitable rewards.

In addition, there is a providential blessing on Joseph's life. That is why we read, *"The Lord was with Joseph so that he prospered, and he lived in the house of his Egyptian master"* (Genesis 39:2). Furthermore, God is going a step further with this providential blessing. The fifth verse of that same chapter says, *"From the time he [Potiphar] put him [Joseph] in charge of his household and of all that he owned, the Lord blessed the household of the Egyptian because of Joseph. The blessing of the Lord was on everything Potiphar had, both in the house and in the field"* (Genesis 39:5). Evidently, God was prospering Potiphar because of Joseph.

We need to be certain that we understand what is really happening here. Joseph does not get anything out of this prosperity. He is a slave. He is not getting a salary, stock, pension, interest in the company, a raise or a medical plan, and there was no revenue sharing. He is a lowly servant. Yet Joseph maintains an unbelievable attitude, and as God blesses him, those blessings splash around him and nourish the Egyptian who bought him. If that was not incredible enough, Joseph seems to delight in this fact. There seems to be delight that God would bless his hands, his work, his intellect and his energy, even though it is of no personal benefit to himself.

I wonder if I would be like that. In all honesty, I am not certain I would. Would you? How is it possible that Joseph had that attitude? It is because Joseph was willing to start at the bottom and work his way up, even if he was not aware there was an "up" and even if "up" was not up some corporate ladder.

This attitude was also because Joseph refused to be mastered by the material. Joseph was probably in a position where he could have taken full advantage of everything Potiphar owned, and could have ruined Potiphar if he has chosen to do so. He could have had everything Potiphar had, and as we will see shortly, he could even have had Potiphar's wife. Yet Joseph refuses to be mastered by the material and the physical, and his success ultimately was for one reason alone, according to Scripture: The Lord was with Joseph.

The secret to your and my success (and ultimately to embracing forgiveness) is having God with us and our being obedient. Think about this: Without a faith-building sermon series to listen to, without a mega-church to be inspired by, without a name-it-and-claim-it preacher to sit under, without a single motivational seminar to go to, without a smoke machine in a worship center and a loud praise band to exhilarate and create emotional responses, and without a book on leadership to read, this man takes a situation under which most of us might crumble and he turns it into an incredible success. I want to know, where did you learn that, Joseph? At what point in your life did this happen and what caused it?

Having examined Joseph's maturity, we are told now of another aspect of his personal makeup that we have not been aware of until now. His wisdom has been dramatically presented, but we learn now that he is handsome, too. Moses describes Joseph's physical characteristics: *"So Potiphar left everything he had in Joseph's care; with Joseph in charge, he did not concern himself with anything except the food he ate. Now Joseph was well-built and handsome ..."* (Genesis 39:6). In other words, Joseph was a hunk! He was a good-looking young man.

So here is the scenario: Joseph is a success in his work. Everything in Potiphar's house is under Joseph's care, *and* Joseph has a handsome face, a ripped body, a youthful and manly appearance, and Potiphar's wife says, "I want one of those!"

This raises a very interesting point: Is success the fertile soil in which temptation can be rooted, where it finds the ideal nutrients to grow? It can be. Many a young man heading for success has been derailed by temptations that seem to lie in greater abundance around the successful rather than around the less successful. Joseph is about to face the most difficult test a young man his age (or any age) can experience, and that is this: A wealthy, seductive, attractive, prominent, mature woman who pursues him. Many a man would sell his birthright and his soul in exchange for this mess of pottage. Kings have gone to war over their desire for such lasciviousness, and Potiphar's wife is luring Joseph into *immediate* sexual gratification.

Why do you suppose Potiphar's wife makes such advances? It is widely known that men are the ones who usually make aggressive, sexual moves on women. Here the circumstances are reversed. As the story of Joseph's experience unfolds, there is something further that we will notice about Potiphar's household. There is a subtle clue as to why his wife might have had eyes for Joseph. A more careful scrutiny of verse 6 reveals an intriguing thought. The verse is presented here once again: "**So Potiphar left everything** he had in Joseph's care; with Joseph in charge, **he did not concern himself with anything** except the food he ate ..." (Genesis 39:6a).

Could it be that Potiphar is neglectful of everything, including his wife? He has left everything in Joseph's care, and he pursues his career; he loses himself in his work and becomes inattentive at home. The interesting thing about this verse is that it indicates that the only thing Potiphar cared about was his food. Potiphar is evidently a selfish man. His behavior borders on narcissism. I suspect there are needs in Mrs. Potiphar's life that her husband is neglectful of, and these are subtle set-ups for the ensuing confrontation with Joseph. This is a warning for us to be watchful of our homes.

Temptation often comes unexpectedly. I am sure Joseph did not see this coming. However, as temptation progresses, it becomes unrelenting. Reading further in the account, we are told, *"And though she spoke to Joseph day after day, he refused to go to bed with her or even be with her"* (Genesis 39:10). Notice the phrase, "... *day after day* ..." She did not give up. This was not a one-time encounter. The adverbial phrase "day after day" implies that she returned every day to persuade, cajole and tempt him. She was unrelenting. Perhaps she would figure out ways to lure him into the room where she was. Perhaps she would find ways to be alone with him for just a minute or two. She would walk past him. She would whisper in his ear. She would brush up against him, and she would do this consistently. That is the subtle temptation and the set-up that Satan has on the agenda for each one of us as God's children, and in fact for every human being – especially in this age of social media.

This kind of temptation is often meant to be secretive, and it can be incredibly subtle. It is possible that the attention appealed to Joseph's ego and his need for affection after being alone, mistreated and abandoned for so long. It may have caused great confusion as he tried to reconcile all that had happened to him with his faith in God. It would have been rather easy for him to cave in to this temptation, just as many do today.

At some point, temptation reaches the point of decision. Believe me, child of God, you can be certain that Satan will push temptation to this point. There is something that I want to say here that I will repeat later: *Sin never delivers what temptation promises.*

That decisive moment in Joseph's life has now arrived. The man he has grown to be so far will show itself in this crucial moment. Never could he have dreamed that what he thought were private temptations would be placed on this "world stage", read about and discussed centuries later. Every time a believer or an inquirer picks up a Bible to read his story, his temptations and decisions are made public once again. Our temptations and decisions may not be made public as Joseph's are, but they will be brought before us at the judgment seat of Christ.

On a particular day, Mrs. Potiphar approaches Joseph like all the other times, only this time she is excessively urgent and insistent that he come to bed with her, and her forceful tugging at him implies that she wants him now, and she is demanding it.

The touch of a woman on any part of a man's body, even hands and arms, carries an immediate draw that sends signals to every nerve ending of his body in a way that words do not. For women, often the draw is through words, but a man is never as weak as when an attractive woman touches him in a sensual way. This is the temptation that Potiphar's wife puts before Joseph, and his response will be the determining factor for his future and the fate of the Hebrew nation. There is no way he can know the consequences of his decision, but we can be sure of one thing; there are always consequences. Will Joseph react or will he act? Will he react to sin and temptation as Reuben, Judah and his other brothers did, or will he turn the tide and set a new course?

With a sudden tug away from her, he flings himself in an about-face, and runs. As she grabs hold of him, he moves away so fast that all she can grab is a bit of his clothing. He quickly wriggles free from the garment, leaving its empty sleeves in her hands. Now left with nothing but a part of his garment, her lustful passions cool and crystalize into resentment, anger and a desire for revenge.

Joseph, on the other hand, with his heart racing and perspiration prickling his skin, can be pictured, perhaps leaning against a tree trying to catch his breath after running so hard. Surely he must know that what he did was right? Ralph Elliot gives an overview of the scenario.

> In spite of the fact that Joseph was far from home in the midst of the lax moral life of Egypt, he was able to withstand the test. Strength was his, for he somehow had been able to maintain a consciousness of the presence of the Lord. Better than his father Jacob before him, he was stalwart in the recognition that to sin against the trust of a human relationship was to sin against God. Joseph may have had more than his share of egotism, but he also had a strong moral code which forbade his participation in lustful wickedness. He may have lost his garment but he refused to lose his innocence and fled from the scene of temptation.
>
> In his relationship with his brothers it had been the lack of practical judgment which baited enmity, but in the trial by sensual pleasure it was the wisdom of practical action which preserved him. The experiences of life were gradually preparing Joseph for the fulfillment of his place in the covenant preservation.[24]

Joseph's first sexual temptation: Complete. His result? Passed. Lesson learned? Yes! But this is only the beginning! Once again, Joseph loses a coat, but he is fast exchanging those garments for a kingdom about which he knows nothing yet.

---

24   Ralph H. Elliott, *The Message of Genesis* (Nashville TN: Broadman Press, 1961), 182.

LESSONS LEARNED IN ANOTHER DYSFUNCTIONAL HOUSEHOLD

Somewhere in Joseph's life he has learned something that prepared him for this event. We don't know when or where it happened, but Joseph knew his place in Potiphar's household, and he knew how to respond appropriately to the inappropriate. What is more, Joseph had the courage to take a stand. He was very well aware that he was in the midst of sexual temptation, and he knew he must reject the woman's advances.

When temptation comes, it not only affects the physical. Temptation's major attack is on the emotional and spiritual makeup of a person. The following are some basic observations about Joseph:

Joseph resists the temptation. It is interesting to note that the decision to reject Potiphar's wife seems to have been made before he runs away. We see no moment of indecision, of entertaining the temptation. Somewhere in his past, he has already prepared for this moment. He may have decided on his standard years ago, or perhaps it came through days of being bombarded with her advances. But he came to certain decision and stuck to it, as we see in Genesis 39:8–9, which says, *"But he refused. 'With me in charge,' he told her, 'my master does not concern himself with anything in the house; everything he owns he has entrusted to my care. No one is greater in this house than I am. My master has withheld nothing from me except you, because you are his wife. How then could I do such a wicked thing and sin against God?'"* In Joseph's handling of this situation, he displays several qualities already apparent in his life.

His character is revealed. The pronouns in the eighth verse are stunning. He uses *me*, *my, my, I, me* and *I* again. It is as if Joseph is saying, "I have a responsibility here. Your husband has given me care of everything in this house. It is on me! It is my responsibility! I am responsible for everything that happens in this situation, and I will not dishonor him because if I did, I would be dishonoring God." It is as if the situation looks to him almost beyond his control, but he retains a strong sense of identity and of responsibility throughout the temptation, and so wins through. He knows what he has to do. He is responsible for how he acts towards his master's wife, and he knows this all too well.

His personal sense of conviction is established. As verse nine clearly demonstrates, somewhere in Joseph's life he has learned that all sin is a sin against God. Now that he is called on to take a stand, his personal conviction reigns supreme, unlike in his brothers' cases where convictions quickly crumbled in the face of temptation. Joseph and his brothers had been raised in the same family but showed completely different responses to life's challenges. He is a living example of 1 Thessalonians 4:3–8, which teaches that the child of God is to flee sexual immorality.

Joseph's rejection of Potiphar's wife will cause further rejection for him. Joseph did right. No question about it. But the question I have for Joseph is this: "Did you think you might receive a reward, some sort of vindication from slavery or a higher status because of the godly stance you took? What did you think would happen when Mrs. Potiphar became indignant because of her pride? Certainly you could not have foreseen the backlash you were about to encounter." Joseph will learn a valuable lesson very soon, and it is the same lesson that each of us must learn. It forms part of the forgiveness that we are called upon to extend; that when we take a stand for godly values, those outside of God's will often create havoc for the one walking inside His will.

Why do people do this? In thinking about why the wife of Potiphar would put Joseph in this situation, I would like to raise the question to her: "Mrs. Potiphar, why the revenge? What was the pay-off for you? Why did you not just repent before Joseph and the Lord, asking them for forgiveness and never speak another word about it to anyone in the house? It would have been over! Done!"

Isn't it interesting that when we tell the truth, everything falls into its proper place – in the past. But when we lie, those lies establish themselves firmly in our future. Why do we not repent immediately after we sin? Solomon Schimmel gives a little insight into these matters:

There are many reasons that we find it hard to repent. The most obvious, perhaps trivial, one is that we do not repent, but instead repeat our sins for the same reasons that we committed them in the first place. We are arrogant, wrathful, envious, lazy, lustful, gluttonous, and greedy, and because of these traits we sin against others. It isn't easy to eliminate or significantly modify a trait, no matter if we were born with it or acquired it later. So we become repeat offenders.

We commit offenses because they are gratifying, and they remain gratifying even though we know that we were wrong for committing them. So we commit them again. Some people are elevated when they tread upon others. Sex is so intensely pleasurable that kings have gone to war in order to acquire a woman they desire.[25]

With that explanation, Potiphar's wife is exposed, along with every human being that has ever lived. In order to cover up her trespass, she unleashes her wrath upon Joseph. As a result, Joseph is soon to experience another travesty of justice; being in Egypt against his will was a travesty to begin with, and now, in evoking the wrath of Potiphar's wife, he is about to be wrongfully jailed. Often, there is great animosity towards those who expose the truth or attempt to live with godly character. Joseph will feel the heat of those who are defiantly wicked and opposed to the will of God.

STANDING DOWN TEMPTATION

What is the number one predator of humans in America? Some might jokingly say it is government, but truthfully, it is the mountain lion. Though Craig Childs is a naturalist and evolutionist, he studies mountain lions, and I want to include him in this story because I think his experience provides a powerful illustration of what I want us to understand.

While in the Blue Range Wilderness, Childs was stalking and studying mountain lions throughout the western part of the United States. In his book, *The Animal Dialogues: Uncommon Encounters in the Wild,* he wrote about an unexpected encounter he had while in Arizona with one of these dangerous beasts.

---

25 Solomon Schimmel, *Wounds Not Healed By Time* (New York, NY: Oxford University Press, 2002), 170-171.

While out walking, he came upon a mountain lion drinking from a lake. The lion did not see him. He watched as it drank and then disappeared back into the woods. He waited a little while, then walked to where the lion had been, hoping to measure the paw prints to discover the lion's size and take some notes. He was just about to bend down, when he thought he should look up and make sure there was nothing in front or behind him. As he did so, about thirty feet away, he saw a pair of eyes looking right back at him. He recounts the story:

Mountain lions are known to take down animals six, seven, and eight times their size. Their method? Attack from behind, clamp onto the spine at the base of the prey's skull, and snap the spine. The top few vertebrae are the target, housing respiratory and motor skills that cease instantly when the cord is cut.

I held firm to my ground and did not even intimate that I would back off. If I run, it is certain that I will have a mountain lion all over me. If I give it my back, I will only feel it briefly as his weight pushes me against the ground. The canine teeth will open my vertebrae without breaking a single bone.

The mountain lion begins to move to my left, and I turn keeping my face on it. My knife in my right hand, it paces to my right trying to get around me and to my other side to get behind me. I turn to the right staring at it. My stare is about the only defense I have. The lion moved back to my left and back to my right, coming closer and closer until it got within ten feet of me trying to get me to do everything but stand there and stare at him.

The mountain lion wanted me to spin around and run so that he could attack me from behind, but when I would not do that after thirty minutes, the lion turns and slowly walks away into the mountains, defeated by a man who knew what never to do in its presence.[26]

---

26 Craig Childs, *The Animal Dialogues: Uncommon Encounters in the Wild* (New York, NY: Little Brown and Company, 1997), 63-64.

That is about as good of an illustration as I can find of how a follower of Christ is to stare down temptation. Although Joseph physically fled, using a figure of speech, we can say he stared down raw temptation. Figuratively, he did not flinch, praise the Lord. I think some key thoughts for the Christian to learn from Joseph are as follows:

I. REALIZE HOW SUBTLY SATAN OPERATES IN TEMPTATION

Satan is a roaring lion. He is a predator of the body, the emotions, the psyche, the spirit and the soul. He wants every part of our being. If he cannot have the believer's soul, his goal is to keep the believer as miserable and unproductive as he can in order to destroy our earthly life and witness, thus gaining a foothold so that no more unbelievers become followers of Christ. He desires that you and I be so miserable and unproductive as Christians so that we will discourage others from coming to know Jesus as their Lord and Savior. Satan is subtle. He is on the prowl.

II. SATAN LAUNCHES ATTACKS OF TEMPTATION SUDDENLY AND UNEXPECTEDLY

That is the reason that the child of God must nail down his or her commitment to the Lord *before* temptation arrives. You and I cannot wait until after temptation has arrived to make that commitment. Just like Craig Childs, we must already know what to do prior to meeting up with trouble. Concealment is on Satan's agenda. He will hide!

III. SATAN CAUSES TEMPTATION TO BE UNRELENTING

Always remember that just because you have won the victory, that does not mean the war is over. The battle might be won, but others will follow. I assure you, temptation will always be on Satan's agenda. He will be back.

IV. SATAN CAUSES SIN TO APPEAR SECRETIVE

The greatest lie Satan wants the child of God to believe is that sin will not harm our soul. A common lie closely associated with that is that nobody will ever find out. Maybe for a while that will be true, but woe to a person who is living in secret sin, especially when their spouse is praying,

"Dear Lord, if there is something I need to know, please allow me to find out." Scandal is on Satan's agenda. He will expose.

V. SATAN CAUSES TEMPTATION TO BE SUBTLE

Sin appeals to all five of the senses. It feels good. It looks good. It sounds good. It tastes good, and it may even smell good. More than that, it may seem right. In the end, it is intended by the enemy to be deadly. That is what is on the blueprint of Satan. My former statement is worth repeating: *Sin never delivers what temptation promises.* Subtlety is on Satan's agenda. He will disguise temptation as something beneficial. He will lie.

VI. SATAN WILL USE OUR PRIDE AGAINST US

Have you ever known a rather proud person who says, "That could never happen to me. I would not let it happen. I'm not that kind of person!" It may be true that you desire never to entertain temptation or to fall into sin. It is not in your heart to make those mistakes. Most people do not wake up in the morning and think, "You know what? I choose to fall into sin today." That is not how sin usually gets us.

Satan has attacked many people who thought they would never fall into sin. We must remain always on the alert. If we do not, we easily allow ourselves to "walk too close to the precipice" of temptation, always believing *WE* are not the kind to fall, *WE* will never make the mistake others have made, and *WE* are strong enough to handle it. Many have made that mistake, shocked at how their pride lied to them. Pride is one of Satan's favorite tools. Humiliation of our pride is on Satan's agenda. He will deceive.

VII. RECOGNIZE THAT RETRIBUTION IS ON ITS WAY WHEN TEMPTATION IS REJECTED

What else can we learn about temptation? Rejected temptation always has residual effects. As a child of God, you will face retribution in some way in your life. This is a certain truth. Furthermore, the retribution will not be pleasant. Potiphar's wife told Joseph to lie with her, and he fled.

Consider this phrase, "staring down temptation". It may be different to what you think. Do not confuse "staring down temptation," with literally standing in front of obvious sin and staring at it. Consistently gazing on sin, entertaining sinful thoughts, lustfully looking at wickedness will obviously lead you in the wrong direction, as King David found to his own regret after staring at Bathsheba while she was bathing. The term "staring down" is a metaphor for a heart attitude of refusing to engage in sin, no matter what the temptation. If it involves physically walking or running away, so be it. Believers must flee from sin; that is why the Christian is told to flee fornication (1 Corinthians 6:18).

However, just because one does the right thing and flees, that does not mean trouble is over. Trouble may well pursue the child of God. Have you noticed that when the lustful advances of people who blatantly disregard the Lord are rejected, they often erupt into unbelievable rage in order to cover their sin?

When we encounter this, we need to understand what really drives that rage. The rage that Potiphar's wife shows may well be felt for her husband, although she directs it at Joseph. When she screams in verse 14, she reveals, perhaps without realizing it, that she blames the whole incident on Potiphar. Listen to her words in the New King James Version: *"... she called to the men of her household and said to them, 'See, he [Potiphar] has brought in a Hebrew to us to make sport of us; he came in to me to lie with me, and I screamed'"* (Genesis 39:14 NKJV).

The woman was rejected, and her first instinct is to blame the whole thing on her husband for having brought Joseph into the house. Interestingly, she does not use the term, "my husband" but refers to him as "Potiphar". I am convinced she is resentful. She is obviously upset with Joseph, but not as furious with him as she is with her husband. He is an inattentive husband leading a dysfunctional household, and she is mad at him. It is also clearly pointed out that Potiphar and Joseph are not the only men in the house. She called out to the other men in the house, indicating that Potiphar is not really the man of the house. We can conclude that this may not have been her only seduction attempt, but it may have been her first rejection.

This stands as an example to us that if rejected lust turns into wounded rage, it is often directed at the innocent. When we reject temptation, persecution may follow because we have refused to join another in their responses to their own dysfunctional home or work life. When passion is disturbed, tempers often rage. It is not fair, yet we are called upon to forgive.

You may recall that Simon Peter warned the churches of Asia Minor that persecution could be the result of doing right. Peter said, *"But how is it to your credit if you receive a beating for doing wrong and endure it? But if you suffer for doing good and you endure it, this is commendable before God" (1 Peter 2:20).*

The Word of God does not say that when right is executed troubles will end. God never seeks to mislead us and paint a picture more rosy than the reality we will face. The Scriptures at no point imply that pure motives will be respected and honored. Sometimes a life of being misunderstood is a learned ministry for us. However, the good news is that man's response is not God's final answer and has nothing to do with God's favor.

The Lord was with Joseph, and as the story progresses, the Lord is still with Joseph. Yet, how much more can one man take? Penitentiary exit: Turn right!

CHAPTER FOUR

JOSEPH'S DEFINING MOMENTS
IN A DETENTION FACILITY

What thoughts go through the mind of a convicted felon as he sits in a bus, making its way to the penitentiary? The bus finally pulls into the prison grounds, comes to a complete stop, and the prisoner knows he is home, a place where he will spend the next several years of his life. What is he thinking? Perhaps he asks, "Could life get any worse?" Imagine how Joseph must have felt in a foreign land as he is thrown into prison, accused of a crime that he did not commit.

Whatever Joseph thought about his future while still traveling to Egypt, whatever fears he may have harbored, they are unlikely to have included a criminal charge and jail. How could his promising start end like this? When a person goes to prison for a crime he commits, there may be remorse or even repentance; just imagine the despair of being accused of something you have not done, of being in a country you hardly know, where you have no friends or relatives, and where all are predisposed to dislike and suspect you.

Try to imagine, if you can, what it must be like to arrive at a prison to serve a sentence for which you are completely innocent. I have visited many prisons in my ministry, and every time I arrive at one, I think of what that must be like. Just the thought of it is almost unbearable.

We read nothing of the trial of Joseph after Mrs. Potiphar's indiscretion against him, and we read nothing of a jury or a judge. Imagine feeling abandoned, even seemingly by God!

On the cross, Jesus felt that type of abandonment as the heavenly Father turned His back on His Son while He was bearing the weight of the world's sin. Yet even Jesus knew that in the final analysis He would be restored to the glory He once had. He previously had told his disciples that he would be killed and be resurrected on the third day (Mark 8:31). Yet at least He knew that there was going to be glorification and eternal redemption for all those who would trust in Him in the end. But from an earthly viewpoint and from our finite vision, Joseph had no such comfort at this time. Is this too much for one man to bear? For some men, possibly. Will Joseph pass this further test of character?

History is full of martyrs who have been killed for their faith, bearing on their shoulders the wrath of ungodly men, paying for crimes they did not commit. In the 105th Psalm, David writes of this injustice as it related to Joseph. *"He called down famine on the land and destroyed all their supplies of food; and he sent a man before them – Joseph, sold as a slave. They bruised his feet with shackles, his neck was put in irons, till what he foretold came to pass, till the word of the Lord proved him true"* (Psalm 105:16–19).

DISASTER IS PILED UPON INJUSTICE

When we saw Joseph last, he was running away from a wild woman, trying to escape her advances as fast as he could. Although she put the moves on him, he remained steadfast in his integrity and commitment. This went on day after day, possibly week after week, and maybe month after month. How long, we are not told. By the time the reader arrives at Genesis 39:10, she is an incredibly frustrated woman. It says, *"And though she spoke to Joseph day after day, he refused to go to bed with her or even be with her"* (Genesis 39:10). No doubt she saw to it that she would badger him every single day. She is now at the point that her reputation, pride and ego is on the line, and she is going to have him no matter what. Fortunately, he resists. Consequently, she is furious.

Potiphar's wife screams and tells all of the other male servants her fabricated story; that Joseph tried to force himself on her. When her husband comes home, she further unloads on him. Potiphar throws Joseph in the king's prison, and we almost want to say, "God, what is going on here? He took a stand for what is right. Why is it that time and time again he is knocked down?" Initially there is very little answer to those questions. Joseph has enormous baggage from the past to sort through, the least of which are his issues with Potiphar and his wife. More fundamental than any dismay he may be feeling about recent events is his confusion about the entire course his life has taken; the forced wrench from his family, the shocking change from favorite son to slave in a foreign country. He has much to work through.

Call it, *"Lessons Learned in the Pit,"* or *"The Place of Preparation,"* or whatever you may think is fitting, but he is certainly not ready for the place of promotion.

Just because we endure hardship as Scripture calls for us to do (2 Timothy 2:3), that hardship does not automatically qualify us for the type of promotion Joseph will eventually obtain. Contrary to the belief contained in a popular phrase, "trials make the man," trials do not make the man. It is the lessons learned and wisdom gained, later assimilated into real life experiences from those trials that help to make the child of God. Trials without learning accomplish little. Joseph clearly uses every experience as a learning opportunity, and as a result he matures into the forgiving man God intends for him to be.

In circumstances such as the ones Joseph finds himself in, it is easy to blame God. The brothers are not there to blame. They have moved on with their lives. Potiphar and his wife are no longer around to take the blame. Sitting in a dungeon, the soul's anguish might easily cause a person in such circumstances to rail against God, blaming Him for these injustices. Paul J. Meyer gives thought to this dilemma.

> You have to come to a point in your life where you can say, "I don't understand what happened, but I still trust you, God." And if necessary, and, "I forgive you, God. Please heal me."
>
> It will do you good to say it. Though technically you cannot forgive God because He is not responsible for your hurt or pain, it can do you good emotionally, spiritually, and mentally to tell Him that you forgive Him. If it helps you, then by all means do it.
>
> As you know, the person who loses is the person who gets bitter. Release any bitterness that you have toward God. If you don't, it will drive a wedge between you and Him. Your relationship will stagnate

and you will be miserable. And like a bothersome neighbor, you will try to avoid God at all costs.[27]

Meyer makes some good observations, and it is true that when our relationship stagnates with God, we will try to avoid His counsel and put off embracing His forgiveness or extending it to others. Yes, there are some good points that Meyer makes. His theology might, however, be somewhat lacking. As we have already discussed, telling God that we forgive Him should not be necessary. Quite frankly, it is impossible because God has no need to be forgiven of anything by anybody. Meyer's point is well taken as he seems to imply that the exercise may be psychologically helpful, although I believe theologically unnecessary. Further help is given from Johann Christoph Arnold.

> When we speak of forgiveness, we usually speak of forgiving the hurts we do to each other, or of God forgiving our sins. But there are times when we accuse God, when we hold him responsible for allowing us to suffer without apparent reason or justification. We rebel and cry out: how can a merciful God permit this? We refuse to accept our lot, and turn away from him in bitterness.

> Can we 'forgive' God? The answer lies in opening our hearts to accept his will. Even if God allows us to suffer, I don't believe that it is his will to hurt us. Rather, he seems to let us endure trials – at times long and difficult periods of anguish – in order to make us turn to him. When we are able to do this humbly, without anger or bitterness, his purpose for us will often become clear.[28]

One proof that Joseph was not overtaken by blaming God is that God's hand is clearly still on him while in prison. He may have had a twinge or two where he breathed, "Why God?" but if he did, we are not told of it. The verification that he was not overtaken with a blasphemous spirit of "God-blaming" was his ability not only to dream, but correctly interpret dreams. In fact, while in prison, Joseph is promoted – and not just in a status sense.

27 Paul J. Meyer, *Forgiveness ... The Ultimate Miracle* (Orlando, FL: Bridge-Logos, 2006) 59.

28 Johann Christoph Arnold, *Seventy Times Seven: The Power of Forgiveness* (Farmington, PA: The Plough Publishing Home, 1997) 114.

Before Pharaoh pardoned and promoted Joseph, God promotes him from a dreamer to an interpreter of dreams. Herbert Lockyer alludes to this fact:

> Joseph the interpreter of dreams proved that prison walls do not a prison make. He acknowledged his dependence upon God for illumination, proving that he was not a mere dreamer but an interpreter of dreams.[29]

I am of the belief that such a promotion could not have happened if God and Joseph had been at odds. Joseph isn't sitting in a cold jail cell in isolation, wondering what God is up to. Joseph is about his Father's business of seeing beyond all of the misfortune. He is dreaming dreams the Lord gives him and interpreting the dreams of others correctly in spite of the isolation.

But is Joseph ready for promotion? Hardly! Is Joseph aware that such a promotion will eventually come? Probably not. As Joseph sits and ponders his future, based on his past experiences, it is hard to believe that he envisions a life of anything but failure.

What Joseph will soon find out is that God does not need ideal situations in which to work. Humans do, but God does not. We want things right. We want excellence. Although God is concerned about every detail of our lives, the lack of perfect details does not hinder His work. He had Joseph in prison. John Bunyan was in a prison when he wrote his famous *Pilgrim's Progress*. Martin Luther was locked up in a room in Wartburg Castle, and John Leland was put in a county jail in Virginia. It is during those times that God often begins His best work.

The day I finally discovered that God does not need me to get all my ducks in a row, and that He could work with me even though my life did not portray the best disciple who ever lived, I finally relaxed, knowing that I had always been in His care. The same is true for you. He can still use you even when others think that you are washed up and even when your life does not fit in with the establishment or the organization's plans – even when your life does not resemble the pedigree and the legacy that others

---

29 Herbert Lockyer, *All the Men of the Bible* (Grand Rapids, MI: Zondervan Publishing House, 1958) 202.

seem to have. It makes no difference when others say you are disqualified. God is the One responsible for your calling in life, not anyone else. You are useful to the Kingdom enterprise regardless of what pharisaical types may think. God can still work even in the midst of the most difficult circumstances in your life. Just trust Him.

As we will see later on, favor comes upon Joseph once again as the jailer puts the prisoner in charge. Favor, in fact, never leaves Joseph. Perhaps it was just put on pause for a while. Now Joseph will acquire cell mates, in whose lives he plays a very prominent role.

These are the broad strokes of his experiences to this point; we will discuss the details a little later on. Let us look at some key points that emerge from the story so far, and how lessons learned in prison become for Joseph defining moments that shape so much of his future career.

GOD PREPARES US IN IMPERFECT SITUATIONS

The reason it is so important to study what happened to Joseph while in prison is that we so often think our own circumstances are not perfect enough for God to work in, thereby discounting possibilities of future miracles. R.T. Kendall demonstrates the purposes of difficult and imperfect situations with reference to Joseph:

> As the saying goes, "Hell hath no fury like a woman scorned." She accused Joseph of rape. Potiphar had Joseph put in prison. Joseph was punished for doing the right thing!
>
> This was the beginning of a period of preparation for Joseph. He didn't realize it at the time, but God had great plans for him. Dr. Martin Lloyd-Jones, my predecessor at Westminster Chapel, used to say to me, "The worst thing that can happen to a man is to succeed before he is ready." God wanted to ensure that Joseph did not come out of prison and embark on the next phase of his life's work until he was ready.[30]

---

30 R.T. Kendall and Joel Kirkpatrick, *Total Forgiveness Experience* (Lake Mary, FL: Charisma House, 2004) 40.

In imperfect situations, God is busy preparing us for what is to come. We cannot see His plans; all we see is the hardship and struggle we face. Do not let this hardship detract you from a truth that lies in this very difficult situation you face, and that is how God may be preparing you for something better.

IMPERFECT SITUATIONS CAN BE A PLACE OF GOD'S PROTECTION

Genesis 39:20 reaches out and grabs the reader's attention. Not only is the word *prison* or *jail* used twice for emphasis, but it becomes obvious that Joseph is in prison for his own protection. Verse 19 says that Potiphar's anger burned, but interestingly enough, it does not tell us at whom this burning rage is directed.

From verse 3 of chapter 39, we can deduce that Potiphar knew the hand of the Lord was on Joseph. Potiphar knew that Joseph was blessed, therefore I speculate (and believe) that his anger is directed at his wife. The more obvious interpretation is that he was angry with Joseph; but when I ponder more deeply on the passage, I become convinced that Potiphar is angry with his wife. He knew what kind of woman she was, and her behavior with Joseph may have been part of a pattern. He may well have had problems with her in the past, but he may also have thought, "I am an official for the king of Egypt. I am in Pharaoh's cabinet, and I must save face."

So Potiphar threw Joseph in the king's prison. Look at this verse: *"Joseph's master took him and put him in prison, the place where the king's prisoners were confined"* (Genesis 39:20a). What did you notice there?

Potiphar is the king's executioner. He could have had Joseph killed on the spot, yet Joseph is put in a prison that is reserved for high-ranking officials who have done wrong– a minimum security political prison. It might have been not as bad as some of the places he could have been sent to.

The question arises, however; who does Joseph need protection from? Probably from Potiphar's wife. While the world may think Joseph is in prison for committing a crime, from God's perspective, he is in there for protection. In this minimum security prison he is safe, watched, cared for, and away from the place of temptation. He is also safe from anything else she might try to do to him.

GOD'S PROMOTES IN IMPERFECT SITUATIONS

One day, the king's cupbearer and the king's baker join Joseph in prison. For some unknown reasons, these men have offended Pharaoh and find themselves now in the same predicament as Joseph.

The cupbearer and the baker have dreams, both of which Joseph interprets. Briefly, Joseph correctly interprets that the cupbearer will live and be restored to his job and the baker will lose his life via execution. Soon, these exact events take place. The baker is executed and the cupbearer is pardoned and returns to work for Pharaoh.

On a particular evening, Pharaoh is troubled by a dream, and his cupbearer tells him of a man he knew in prison who is able to interpret dreams; Joseph. We see that God brought Joseph into contact with someone who would have the ear of Pharaoh at the very time Pharaoh needed the particular skill only Joseph had. You may be realizing my earlier point; God did not need to have Joseph in the halls of Congress. A dungeon would do just fine. It became his place of promotion.

IMPERFECT SITUATIONS ARE A PLACE OF PREPARATION

Psalm 105, as earlier quoted, alludes to the fact that God called for a famine in the land and sent and prepared His own man, Joseph, to advise the king during this time. But first, God prepared and tested him. Joseph may not have liked this preparation. His review might have read, "Didn't enjoy it. Was not fun. Not exactly Club Med. Making no reservations for a return overnight stay!"

The place of our preparation is never a party. It is never a perfect place. Yet in Joseph's case, it was the perfect place for God to break up the fallow ground in his heart so that it would be fertile and ready to embrace forgiveness when the time came. God needed Joseph to mature, to grow into the kind of person who could handle things that even this dreamer had never dreamed possible.

It becomes increasingly clear that every place Joseph goes, he becomes a leader. Jacob wanted Joseph to be a ruler over his brothers. Potiphar makes him ruler over his house. He is the put in the dungeon and the jailers turn the jail over to him. I remember the days of the old television show *The Andy Griffith Show* where, in the make-believe town of Mayberry, North Carolina, Andy turns the keys of the jail over to Otis. There was an episode where Otis, alone in the jail, hears the phone ring; he lets himself out of his cell to answer the phone, then locks himself back up. Joseph's situation is reminiscent of that very thing. Everywhere Joseph goes, people turn everything over to him and place him in charge.

When Joseph looked back on his life in later years, surely he could see that God started preparing him at home and continued his preparation in Potiphar's house and in prison. Later, as we shall see, Pharaoh turns the entire land of Egypt over to him. Each of these situations, while bringing their own hardships and blessings, is also a preparation for the day that Joseph will be re-united with his brothers. Why does God continually promote Joseph? It is because when Joseph is in the place of preparation, he does not whine, cry, kick and scream. He does not try to leave that place of preparation. The Psalmist clearly states, *"He made him master of his household, ruler over all he possessed, to instruct his princes as he pleased and teach his elders wisdom"* (Psalm 105:21–22). Joseph would not have been able to instruct or teach anyone if he had been always trying to escape the place of preparation.

It is the same for you and me. If we keep trying to pray our way out of situations and tasks that are learning experiences for us, we disrupt the preparation that God is attempting.

In the above quoted verse, the Psalmist refers to "princes"; these are Pharaoh's equivalent of senators – the ruling body of priests in Egypt who ran everything. Is it not incredible that Joseph, a monotheistic Jew, is eventually appointed to teach the most educated people in the known world at that time about the wisdom of God? There is a discipline in the life of this young man that causes him to accept the place of preparation; a discipline rarely seen in people today. We need to remember that true leadership never comes without first dwelling in the place of preparation.

The language of the text suggests that the prison where Joseph was incarcerated with the cupbearer and the baker was possibly overseen by Potiphar and may have been connected to his house. At any rate, God did not let Joseph get too far from Potiphar for the simple fact that Potiphar was needed to care for and meet Joseph's needs. Regardless of how unpopular my theory is, my sincere belief is that although Potiphar was a pagan from a foreign land, he had common sense. I think he knew better than to believe his wife's story.

Another theory about which one may only speculate: I have often wondered if Potiphar might have been the "boss" of the chief jailer where Joseph was placed. Perhaps when Joseph was thrown into that prison, Potiphar informed the jailer of Joseph's administrative abilities. Although this detail is mere speculation, we do know that God often works through unbelievers in order to accomplish His will.

FOCUSING ON WHAT WE CAN DO INSTEAD OF WHAT WE CANNOT DO

Like Joseph, in difficult situations we need to learn to focus on what we can do, not on what we cannot do. Note these verses from Genesis 39: *"So the warden put Joseph in charge of all those held in the prison, and he [Joseph] was made responsible for all that was done there. The warden paid no attention to anything under Joseph's care, because the Lord was with Joseph and gave him success in whatever he did"* (Genesis 39:22–23).

Joseph had skills he could use, despite his situation. He could administrate, organize and care for people. He had done that for his father Jacob, who was arguably one of the wealthiest men in the Middle East, and he had done the same in Potiphar's house. Now the jailer turns the jail over to him because Joseph obviously does not sit around complaining about injustices. He never picks a night to take the keys of the jail and try to make a run for it. He does not focus on what he cannot do, but on what he can do.

In fact, now that the cupbearer and the baker are in prison with him, Joseph is put in charge of serving them, which means that he ministers to them. He is in prison and responsible for ministering to the needs of the prisoners.

Because of Joseph's new position in the prison, he could have been cocky and said, "I am not doing anything for you! I run this jail. I handle the administration here, and you are going to work for me. You Sir, are a cupbearer. And you Sir, are a baker. Now both of you – get to work!" Joseph did not do that. He focused on serving others, and God used his situation and his willing attitude to build leadership qualities into his life.

FOCUSING ON THE SPIRITUAL INSTEAD OF THE MATERIAL

Think about this: Joseph is a foreigner. He is a slave. What does he own? Nothing. He is new in town, and he is a Jew in the land of Egypt. He has been sold to the Midianites. That is once. He has possibly been resold to the Ishmaelites (or the other way around). That is twice. He has obviously been sold at the border of Egypt. That is three times. No doubt he has been sold when he was on the auction block. Arguably, Joseph could have been sold as many as four times before he laid his head on a pillow at Potiphar's house.

Now Joseph is a prisoner. He is in a place where he cannot claim anything as his own. This is unlike anything he ever knew back home while he was with his father. Under Jacob's roof, he had everything he wanted. He was the apple of his father's eye and he had a coat and a plot of land to prove it.

Yet in Egypt, he turns a profit for Potiphar. He runs an efficient jail *while* in jail, and in all of this, he receives no salary or share of any revenue. God takes everything away from Joseph so that Joseph can focus only his relationship with God.

Why do you suppose Joseph was able to interpret all of those dreams? It was because he did not have anything standing between God and him. Up until this time, Joseph has been a dreamer. Now he is an interpreter of dreams. God is getting ready to kick it up a notch, for the situation Joseph finds himself in strengthens his spiritual resolve. He may have lost his coat (and everything else), but he has no idea of what is headed his way in exchange for that coat.

FOCUSING ON ONE'S OWN ATTITUDE AND NOT THE ATTITUDES OF OTHERS

Imagine what the attitudes and morale are like in a prison, particularly in the days before prison reform. Joseph has terrific interpersonal skills and a great attitude, which he upholds throughout his incarceration. Others may be depressed, despairing, defeated and bitter. Not Joseph. No wonder he is soon running the jail, even while a prisoner. The cupbearer and the baker begin to move in his orbit, to rely on him and look up to him. His attitude attracts and affects them because he has focused on his own attitude and not the attitude of others.

LEARNING TO BE ACCOUNTABLE

Joseph is accountable to three people at the very least; four if Potiphar is included. He is accountable to the jailer. He is accountable to those who have been entrusted into his care – the cupbearer and the baker (and possibly others). And he is accountable to the Lord. He is, no doubt, in a difficult place of preparation, and in that place, God teaches him accountability.

In spite of all these lessons Joseph has learned (and is learning), an incident occurs that makes one realize that Joseph still has a lot of maturing to do before he is ready to embrace forgiveness.

Crucially, if Joseph loses his focus during this next lesson, it will certainly have an impact upon his future relationship with his family and with the Hebrew nation in a way that is devastating – more than he can understand right now. This lesson on resisting bitterness, once learned, becomes the key element that makes his eventual healing and forgiving spirit possible.

RESISTING THE TEMPTATION TO BE BITTER

In the 40th chapter of Genesis, these words are revealed:

"The captain of the guard assigned them to Joseph, and he attended them. After they had been in custody for some time, each of the two men – the cupbearer and the baker of the king of Egypt, who were being held in prison – had a dream the same night, and each dream had a meaning of its own.

"When Joseph came to them the next morning, he saw that they were dejected. So he asked Pharaoh's officials who were in custody with him in his master's house, 'Why do you look so sad today?'

"'We both had dreams,' they answered, 'but there is no one to interpret them.'

"Then Joseph said to them, 'Do not interpretations belong to God? Tell me your dreams'" (Genesis 40:4–8).

There was no Canon of Scripture back then. There was no corpus of law from God at the time, and God would often speak to people through dreams. Joseph interprets the cupbearer's dream and pronounces that in three days he will be set free and put back to work for the king. It is then that Joseph seems to act out of character; he states these words in verses 14 and 15 of the same chapter: *"But when all goes well with you, remember me and show me kindness; mention me to Pharaoh and get me out of this prison. I was forcibly carried off from the land of the Hebrews, and even here I have done nothing to deserve being put in a dungeon"* (Genesis 40:14–15).

I am so struck by these two verses. Up until now, he has never complained. I am not suggesting he is some super-human who does not have emotions like the rest of humanity. On the contrary, I would suspect this of anyone in his plight. But if Joseph has complained like this before, we have not read it. It is not often we hear this tone from him.

Is Joseph playing a "victim card" here or is he just stating the facts of his case? It is unlikely that he has had an arbitrator or lawyer up to this point, and possibly he is being his own advocate. Whatever the case, he asks the cupbearer to remember him before the king, but in verse 23 it is stated that such remembrance does not happen.

Quite possibly, the forgetfulness of the cupbearer may have been intentional. He may have *chosen* to forget Joseph. We are told in Genesis 41:1 that two more years pass. We may conclude that the cupbearer did not want to say anything about the incident, perhaps for fear of reminding Pharaoh of why the cupbearer had been imprisoned in the first place. One day, Joseph will become the second most powerful man in the known world. Yet incredibly, he never berates the cupbearer for forgetting him for so long; never tries to get revenge. The way he deals with his disappointment at the cupbearer – that complete absence of a desire for revenge - seems to foreshadow his eventual forgiveness of his brothers. Although a little more maturation is needed, there is no doubt that God is preparing him, even in this circumstance.

Nevertheless, Joseph's initial words to the cupbearer about his past experiences in verses 14 and 15 that I have just quoted are bothersome to R.T. Kendall:

Joseph had much to be bitter about. His brothers had treated him with cruelty and disdain. Potiphar's wife had falsely accused him. Most maddening of all, God had apparently allowed all of these things to take place. Joseph had many 'offenders' to forgive.

After some time passed, Joseph had company in prison – Pharaoh's cupbearer and baker. While there, each of them had a dream that Joseph offered to interpret. He predicted that the baker would be hanged in three days, but that the cupbearer would get his job back in the same span of time.

But a temptation too great – so it seemed – was handed to Joseph on a silver platter. He had barely finished telling the cupbearer that he would be restored to Pharaoh's favor when Joseph got too involved in his prophetic word. These words (Genesis 40:14-15) prove to us that Joseph needed to be delivered from bitterness and self-pity.[31]

---

31   Ibid., 41.

As Kendall implies, it seems that a little more "seasoning" is in order for the up-and-coming Joseph. Others could afford to be bitter, but not Joseph. Not God's man! Joseph needed to be free from bitterness because God has something great in store for him, something He did not have in store for others. What was Joseph thinking at this time? Could he have pondered, "Okay, let's take an inventory: The cupbearer has forgotten me. Potiphar's wife, well, I *hope* she forgets me. My brothers have long forgotten me, and they wanted to kill me. They probably assume I am dead. Mom must be dead by now, and if Dad is still alive, I wonder if he has forgotten me? Above all else, God, have you forgotten me as well?" Nowhere are we told that this is what he is thinking, but could he really be judged by us if he had been thinking those thoughts? Wouldn't most of us think that way?

ADDITIONAL LESSONS FOR THE BELIEVER IN THE PLACE OF PREPARATION

Have you ever found yourself in a figurative prison – sometimes of your own making -- perhaps sometimes not? Have you ever found yourself pushed and pulled hard into a place of preparation? It is a place many of us know all too well.

In the place of preparation, moments of depression and despair may come. At such times, it is easy to feel forgotten by everyone and feel that God has abandoned us too. And if we do not feel abandoned, we may feel that we are being punished for some sin.

It is true that the Lord chastises – Scriptures bear this out – but when we feel that God has abandoned us, we are mistaken. On the contrary, the amazing fact that is shown in Joseph's story is that Joseph never forgets God and consequently, God never forgets Joseph.

God's man shows himself faithful in the place of preparation, and God never forgets or abandons him. When the child of God finds himself or herself in the place of preparation, the best thing he or she can do is remain there.

Two major thoughts emerge when we consider hard times as a place of preparation for embracing forgiveness. The place of preparation teaches us about God and, in addition, the place of preparation teaches us about ourselves. We need those lessons in order to forgive deeply so that we may adequately shed our earthly robes of prideful colors, and exchange them one day for a Kingdom.

I. THE PLACE OF PREPARATION TEACHES US ABOUT GOD.

Under this heading, there are at least three aspects of God we can learn from Joseph's time in preparation. There are many more from his story, but I want to focus on three aspects of God that we see from Joseph's time in prison and immediately afterwards.

A. *The mysterious ways of God are revealed.* Pharaoh dreams he is standing on the edge of the Nile. He sees seven sleek, fat, and healthy cows grazing in a marshy area. He then sees seven emaciated, ugly, disease-ridden and pitiful cows coming up from the Nile, and they eat the healthy cows.

   The Egyptians believed in evolution long before Darwin ever came on the scene. They believed that life spontaneously generated from the Nile River. This dream has echoes of that belief. In addition, the Egyptians believed in many gods, including a god for domestic beasts and agriculture. The dream is shocking because, of course, cows do not eat cows, or any other meat for that matter. They are herbivores or vegetarians.

   Disturbed by this dream, Pharaoh wakes up, rubs his eyes, and falls back to sleep. He dreams another dream and sees wheat or corn. He sees a great stalk that grows up, and from it, seven fat, full ears of corn. Then he sees a wilted, diseased stalk that grows up with seven ravaged, unhealthy ears of corn, and all of a sudden the unhealthy ears of corn eat the healthy ears of corn.

If Pharaoh was not disturbed by the cows, he certainly is now. He calls in his magicians or occultists who dabble in the world of spirits and demons. Keep in mind that God is doing so much more here than simply working in Joseph's life. Egypt was a country that had long been on God's radar and it would be for some time. God is showing Pharaoh that Egypt's gods are really not God at all.

God often uses the very things that we put our hope and trust in; He confiscates them in order for us to see how fruitless and powerless those things are; thus, the mysterious ways of God.

B. *The marvelous wisdom of God is revealed.* Why could the magicians not help Pharaoh? The reason is that this was not a dream that demonic spirits could interpret. When God speaks, demons have no part in interpreting His words. Satan is powerless to understand God's way or God's wisdom. It is God who decides who interprets His dreams.

Amazingly, by God's own design, there is someone standing next to Pharaoh while he is in this predicament; the cupbearer. The cupbearer knows someone who can interpret dreams. But does he want to run the risk of mentioning his jail time - or is the king in such a state that even the cupbearer wants to help?

Would an Egyptian Pharaoh have even spoken to a common Egyptian, let alone Joseph who was a Jewish foreigner, a slave and a prisoner? Notwithstanding all this, Pharaoh is in such a conundrum that he is willing to listen to the most unlikely source of help – a Hebrew slave and prisoner.

Before the foundations of the world were created, God knew a famine was coming at this time. He knew that His people would starve to death without His intervention. And so He intervened between disaster and His people, something He still does today. Isn't our God wonderful?

God knows that there is going to be a bountiful crop for seven years before the famine, and He wants to get a man there to tell Pharaoh to prepare. If Egypt consumes all the bounty of the seven plentiful years, they will have nothing left for the seven years of famine. But the king needs an interpreter to tell him this. God puts Joseph in slavery in an official's household, which gets him into the right prison, at the right time, with the right people. Now Joseph is within earshot of Pharaoh. Coincidence? Hardly! That is God's marvelous wisdom. God's ways are mysterious and His wisdom is marvelous.

Why did God not just choose an Egyptian official to come up with the interpretation and the plan to conserve the harvest? If an Egyptian had been the one to reveal the dream and the plan, he might not have included the Hebrews in that plan. He might have provided only for his own nation. Remember the promise? God promised to build a nation from Abraham, and that promise was to come through Isaac. Therefore, God wants Jacob's family to get down to Egypt to save them from starvation and preserve the future nation. The revealer of the dream and the plan to counteract its prophecies had to come from Joseph.

Whatever else we may see in this story, we cannot fail to see how God's hand moves over men and nations. He does the same today. When we are discouraged because of things that go on in our government and our country, we should not forget that God knows how to strum the heart strings of people in all governments and countries, even if they do not know Him as their Lord and Savior. God was, and still is, in control.

C. *The miraculous will of God is revealed.* Joseph comes out of the pit and goes to live in the palace of the most powerful man of the most powerful empire on the planet at that time. Pharaoh takes a foreigner and makes him Prime Minister of all Egypt in a matter of hours, and that has to be nothing other than the will of God.

Joseph interprets the dream correctly and then gives Pharaoh instructions that sound like something coming out of the Harvard School of Business. Now there is a plan in place for the protection of the Egyptians *and* the Hebrew race.

Once Joseph had a robe from his father, stripped from him. He had another robe, left in the hands of Potiphar's wife. Now the king gives him a third robe. What is to be thought of our God after all? Does it appear now that Joseph was abandoned and forgotten? No. Yet in the place of preparation this conclusion is not easy. If the child of God will stay put, the place of preparation will teach much about God.

II. THE PLACE OF PREPARATION TEACHES US MUCH ABOUT OURSELVES.

When we look at Joseph's response to prison and his sudden change of fortune when summoned to see Pharaoh, certain aspects of his character become clear. This is helpful in our own lives. Let us look at three things that Joseph demonstrates and see how they teach us about ourselves.

A. *Joseph demonstrates a dedication to the Lord that should be evident in every Christian.* Pharaoh says that he has heard that Joseph can interpret dreams. Joseph responds by saying, *"I cannot do it ... but God will give Pharaoh the answer he desires"* (Genesis 41:16). Joseph could have said, "I've spent a lot of time in prison as a slave, and it's high-time somebody started respecting me. It is about time that someone sees my accomplishments and the gifts that God has given me. Yes Sir, Mr. Pharaoh, you have called the right man." But instead he says, *"I cannot do it ... but God will..."* (Genesis 41:16). Joseph also says in verse 25, *"... God has revealed to Pharaoh what he is about to do"* (Genesis 41:25). Again in verse 28, *"... God has shown Pharaoh what he is about to do"* (Genesis 41:28). And in verse 32, Joseph says, *"The reason the dream was given to Pharaoh in two forms is that the matter has been firmly decided by God, and God will do it soon"* (Genesis 41:32).

Joseph is telling Pharaoh what every child of God should learn and demonstrate, and that is, "I am not important in this whole situation. I am just speaking for God and it is God who has revealed this to you."

What if you and I had that kind of dedication to the Lord, a dedication that does not care who gets the credit or recognition, but that only Jesus Christ be seen and honored? That dedication would do more to mend lives, homes, and families than anything else. Joseph demonstrates a dedication to the Lord.

B. *Joseph demonstrates a godly distinction that should be evident in every Christian.* Notice the word *evident.* Christians should never have to promote themselves, only present Jesus.

The Egyptian pharaohs were actually worshipped as gods. Instead, Pharaoh himself says to his men, *"... Can we find anyone like this man, one in whom is the spirit of God?"* (Genesis 41:38b). Here is a man [Pharaoh] who was led by demonic spirits of hell, yet he recognizes that the Spirit of God in Joseph is different from what he has within himself. The question to you and me is: Are we living life in such a way that non-believers can immediately see the Spirit of God in us?

In Ephesians, the Apostle Paul gives instructions regarding imitating God and allowing the Spirit of God to be seen in us. In the fourth chapter, he writes of the attributes and conduct we should display, closing the chapter with prohibitions, so that we are quite clear of the sort of conduct expected of us. His instructions continue in chapter five with the general injunction that we should practice the "imitation of God." *"Therefore be imitators of God, as beloved children ..."* (Ephesians 5:1 NASB). We are to positively mimic God. W.A. Criswell paints a vivid picture of what mimicking looks like:

One day in the International Airport in New York City waiting for a plane, I met a man who was at the time Governor of Maryland. He is a gifted political leader who delivered the keynote address at the Republican Convention that nominated President Richard M. Nixon. Learning that I was a pastor, he began to talk with me about the things of God and of his family (all who were Methodists). He began to talk about his mother, who must have been a very devout Christian woman. He said, "My mother had an unusual and strange habit. When she went down to the altar to kneel, to take the Lord's Supper, she always took off her jewelry and put it in her purse before she knelt before the Lord. Do you know that in the days passed and I grew up, I found myself taking off my jewelry. I would take off my ring, take off my watch, take off my jewelry when I knelt to take the Lord's Supper. Last Sunday morning, when I knelt to take the Lord's Supper, my teenage boy was kneeling by my side. To my utter amazement, I saw him take off his jewelry – his ring and his watch." That is nothing but imitation. There is no special reason for it. It is indefensible by one who would seek to question why. It is but the fact that the father imitated his mother and he in turn was imitated by his son. How glorious it is to imitate God! That is the most wonderful originality in the world, to copy the Lord.[32]

Obviously, the removal of jewelry prior to communion is not the issue here. Yet the whole scenario is a beautiful picture of being imitators of God. That is what we see in Joseph, and it is not just to impress the king. Everyone who has ever come in contact with Joseph has seen this quality in him, for it is part of his character.

Dr. Criswell further expounds on being an imitator from the fifth chapter of Ephesians:

As children of God's love, Paul says, we are to be *"mimetai"* of God, *"followers"* of God. *"Mimetai,"* our words *"mimic"* and *"imitator"* come from it. As mimeographs, we are to be copies of God, we are to imitate God. What an admonition! And yet, if we love the Lord, we will find ourselves unconsciously loving and following those precious characteristics that we see of God in Christ Jesus.[33]

There is to be something different in the life of the believer. There is to be distinctiveness. There should be something in the Christian that the world can point to and say, "She is obviously a foreigner." "He is of another world." "There is something that marks them as being truly special." It should be so evident that either the lost person would want to inquire further or they would know immediately that the person is

---

32 W.A. Criswell, *Ephesians: An Exposition* (Grand Rapids, MI: The Zondervan Corporation, 1974) 235.

33 Ibid., 235.

a follower of Jesus Christ. Thus, we must ask the question of ourselves every day: "Is there something uniquely distinguishable about my life that tells people that I serve the Lord Jesus? If I am redeemed, I am accountable to display such redemption in my life. Am I doing that?"

C. *Joseph demonstrates a submission to the Lord that should be paramount in every Christian.* A study of Genesis 41:46 reveals that Joseph is probably seventeen years of age when he is sold into slavery. He is thirty years old when he stands before Pharaoh. For thirteen years this young man was a slave, and at least half of that time, if not more, he was a prisoner.

Has life been hard on you? Do you feel like everyone has forgotten and that nobody cares? Do you feel that even God has given up? For thirteen years Joseph had been in God's place of preparation.

Here is the power of accepting and co-operating with God's preparation: After thirteen years of being a slave and a prisoner, Joseph emerges, and immediately, he becomes the second-most powerful man in the most powerful kingdom in the world. He rules until he is one hundred and ten, and then he dies. That is an eighty-year reign. In light of that, thirteen years is a very short period of preparation.

Moses spent his first eighty years in the place of preparation, then served the Lord for forty years. It was either God's plan, or it took Moses eighty years to learn what it took Joseph thirteen years to learn.

It is not always the case, but in most lives, we ourselves determine how long we remain in the place of preparation. Most assuredly, it is always longer than we think it should be. Often we Christians say, "When I finally get out of school and get a job, I'll begin to do what God has called me to do. Until then, I'll do what I want to do," or "When we have children, we'll get involved in church," or "When I begin to see God move, I'll start to think about God. Until then, I deem that God is silent."

Or we question God along the lines of, "When can I get a new job, Lord? When will we feel that our heads are above water?" Our situations are not perfect, and our subconscious response is to say, "I refuse to be God's man or God's woman until God jumps through my hoop." On the contrary, the sovereignty of God means that He has the right to demand anything from the life of His creation, including His redeemed Bride ... and my life!

God often puts His dear children in the place of preparation, not so that He can hear them scream, but so that He might build in them qualities of leadership. That is what he has been doing with Joseph. Joseph is about to come out of the dungeon. How many years has he been there? That is not certain, and it is widely debated. However, when he comes out of that prison, he is going to be placed in a position of incredible power and prominence.

Joseph will not be in that place of authority just to help the Egyptians. God has built into Joseph what he needs and what the Hebrew people need. God has prepared him to save the handful of Jews who would starve if it were not for Joseph's influence.

Joseph is going to deliver the very brethren who rejected and sold him. The one whom the brothers thought they had sent to certain death will be the one who will deliver them from death. In addition, through Joseph's life, God is displaying a forerunner of the coming Messiah.

Oh, my broken-hearted friend, who knows what God can do with you? Who knows what God is going to do when the day of preparation has concluded? When the bus pulls up in the prison yard, the prisoner thinks, "Can it get any worse than this?" My friend, only God knows the answer. Just remember: The last chapter hasn't been written yet.

CHAPTER FIVE

JOSEPH'S DEFINING MOMENTS AS A DISTINGUISHED FINANCIER

There is an old folk idiom that goes something like this: "He who enslaves himself to the compass has the freedom of the seas." Joseph has done just that. He has played by the rules and he has lived out his faith under the most difficult of circumstances, and is now ready to emerge from obscurity. Soon he will be a hero throughout the land of Egypt. He will be placed in a position that ultimately will allow him to be a blessing to his own Hebrew people, as well as to everyone else. Such opportunities have not come to him without serious hardship.

Still a prisoner, Joseph is called to the palace and asked to interpret Pharaoh's dreams. These dreams were briefly outlined in the previous chapter, and needless to say, they were so disturbing that Pharaoh was desperate to acquire help in unraveling them. The dreams were so detailed, so intense and so very strange that Pharaoh knew he could not pass these off as fluke occurrences, nightmares, or the result of too much rich food prior to bedtime. No. These dreams obviously had a purpose, and even being the pagan that Pharaoh was, he knew that something or someone was trying to get his attention.

Genesis chapter 41 is somewhat of a transition chapter, and we should not pass it off as unimportant. Joseph's future hinges on the events in this chapter, as does the future of his brothers, his family and the Hebrew nation.

GIVING GOD THE HONOR: JOSEPH INTERPRETS PHARAOH'S DREAMS
Interestingly, the cupbearer begins to remember Joseph two years after being released from prison. Either he honestly forgot about Joseph, or he is so disturbed by Pharaoh's distress that he is willing to have his negative past recalled just so that Pharaoh might get the help he needs.

It may have been frightening to the cupbearer to remember and introduce Joseph to the king. What if Joseph interpreted the dreams incorrectly? Then the cupbearer would most assuredly find himself executed. The cupbearer might have thought, "Yes, I know that Joseph interpreted the dreams correctly while in prison, but this is Pharaoh, for crying out loud! What if Joseph gets it wrong this time? Is that a chance I want to take?" Consequently, there might have been good motivation for his memory lapse.

It is important to note here that the cupbearer was more than just a bearer of Pharaoh's cup. He brought Pharaoh his food and drink and tasted it prior to Pharaoh consuming it in order to make sure the food and drink was not poisoned; but in addition, he was closer to Pharaoh than any other person. He might have been considered his Chief of Staff. He was within reach of Pharaoh at all times and had Pharaoh's ear. It is safe to say that this cupbearer was a close, trusted advisor to Pharaoh. He lost that position once. He has it back now. Does he want to take a chance on losing it again?

Nevertheless, the cupbearer finally remembers this "dreamer" from prison. Joseph is now brought out of prison, cleaned up, and presented before Pharaoh. This dreamer who now stands in front of the most powerful potentate in the world is about to make the most crucial interpretation of dreams the world has ever known. Joseph's answer will reverberate through the generations and he will be hailed as the greatest dream interpreter of his day or of any day.

Once again, we find Joseph is wearing a new robe. This time he is not a slave. He is not a supervisor, and he is not quite royalty either. That will come later. Nevertheless, after all he has gone through, we see a man emerging here who is beginning to resemble our Lord. Charles Spurgeon sees the resemblance:

This striking likeness of Joseph strongly reminds us of our Master and Lord, that greater Joseph, who is Lord over all the world for the sake of Israel. Peter in his sermon to the household of Cornelius, said of our Lord that He "went about doing good, and healing all that were oppressed of the devil; for God was with Him." Exactly what had been said of Joseph. It is wonderful that the same words should describe both Jesus and Joseph, the perfect Savior and the imperfect patriarch. When you and I are perfected in grace, we shall wear the image of Christ, and that which will describe Christ will also describe us. Those who live with Jesus will be transformed by His fellowship till they become like Him. To my mind, it is very beautiful to see the resemblance between the firstborn and the rest of the family, between the great typical man, the Second Adam, and all those men who are quickened into His life, and are one with Him. [34]

The most striking aspect of Joseph is not his handsome features, which were seen and coveted by Potiphar's wife. What is most revealing of all is the One he resembles. This is the beginning of the "new Joseph."

The future patriarch stands before Pharaoh, and we might think that Joseph would be tempted to say, "Finally! Someone has seen the real me. Yes, Pharaoh, here I am at your service. You have called the right man." Perhaps in earlier days he might say that, but not this day. Joseph quickly shares with the king that the interpretation will come from Jehovah God. Note that Joseph gives God the credit *before* God has even revealed the meaning of the dreams to Joseph. What faith! Joseph correctly interprets the dreams and lets Pharaoh know how to prepare the nation and protect the people from starvation.

Having completed the interpretation, Joseph is probably thinking that his task is over and it is time to head back to prison. Suddenly, Pharaoh turns him on a dime. He promotes him, and in the twinkling of an eye, Joseph becomes the second most powerful man in the world. He has gone from the pit to a pinnacle in a matter of minutes, and I am sure that Joseph never anticipated anything remotely like this. He may have foreseen a life of imprisonment, certainly of enslavement. Instead, having spent ten to twelve years in prison, he is suddenly a free man and more; he is ruler over Pharaoh's affairs, at thirty years of age.

---

34 Charles H. Spurgeon, *The Treasury of the Bible, Vol. 1.* Grand Rapids, MI: Zondervan Books, 1962 reprint) 152.

EQUIPPED TO INSTRUCT A PAGAN CULTURE

Joseph's new position does not cause him to become a changed man. That change had already taken place. Joseph was being forged and molded while in prison, equipped, trained in humility and faith, and made ready for what God had purposed for him. As a result of submitting to the changes God worked within him during those difficult years, he now experiences freedom. F.B. Meyer speaks of the "graduation" Joseph received after difficult years, which all us who are believers may experience:

And what was the result? Joseph was carried through the hatred and opposition of his foes; and his dreams were literally fulfilled in the golden days of prosperity, which came at length. Just as Jesus was eventually seated at the right hand of God, as Prince and Savior. And your time, sufferer, shall come at length, when God shall vindicate your character, and avenge your sorrows. "Trust in the Lord, and do good; fret not thyself in any wise to do evil; for evil-doers shall be cut off: but those that wait upon the Lord, they shall inherit the earth. He shall bring forth thy righteousness as the light, and thy judgment as noonday" (Psalm 34).[35]

There comes a time when God is ready for the curtain to be pulled back, revealing the marvelous maturation work of the Holy Spirit in the lives of each one of us who are His children. Jameson and Fausset explain that this was Joseph's appointed time:

What a long time for Joseph to experience the sickness of hope deferred! But the time of his enlargement was come when he had sufficiently learned the lessons that God designed for him; and the plans of Providence were matured. [36]

It is rather difficult to detail all of the lessons Joseph learned while in prison. As we stated earlier, much about this story is hidden. Details have obviously been omitted for reasons known only to the Holy Spirit. We see,

---

35   F.B. Meyer, *Joseph: Beloved, Hated, Exalted* (New York, NY: Fleming H. Revell Company, Reprint, 1911) 17.

36   Robert Jamieson and A.R. Fausset, *Commentary, Critical and Explanatory on the Old and New Testaments* (Cincinnati, OH: National Publishing Company, 1872) 41.

for instance, that the inner working of the Lord in Joseph's heart is not seen to the extent that it is with Job. All we know is that the Lord was with Joseph, and that the fruit of the cultivation God had accomplished was clearly visible and demonstrated. Whatever God did with Joseph in that place of preparation, it became obvious to Pharaoh that he was not dealing with just any Hebrew, as Theodore Epp explains:

> Even the God-rejecting world of Joseph's day testified that Joseph was a man of God. After Joseph had been brought from prison and had interpreted Pharaoh's dream, "Pharaoh said unto his servants, Can we find such a one as this is, a man in whom the Spirit of God is?" (Genesis 41:38). This phrase fittingly described Joseph, and it was because the Spirit of God was in him that he was able to say after his gross mistreatment by his brothers, "God planned it for good" (50:20, Berkeley).[37]

Although Jacob had been dysfunctional in raising his boys, although his sons treated their half-brother cruelly and unjustly, and although Potiphar's wife was wicked in her own way, while in prison Joseph did not just sit his time out. Perhaps he prayed and asked God to forgive him of *his* failures. Was it possible that Joseph recognized that he had been wrong in his attitudes and in his immature shortcomings? One will never know, but the degree to which Joseph was elevated is certainly commensurate with humility. Furthermore, the degree of his elevation is indisputable proof that Pharaoh was not the one who promoted Joseph, although from a human standpoint, it may appear that way. Rather, God promoted Joseph.

In my ministry, I have had people ask this question on many occasions: "How was it possible for Joseph to emerge from all he went through and still embrace forgiveness as he did?" I cannot prove this, but I firmly believe that the answer is found in what took place within the prison walls during the years of Joseph's incarceration; things that we will never know. In addition, I suspect that whatever happened to mature Joseph, it did not bypass confession and repentance of any sin that was harbored in his heart.

---

37   Theodore H. Epp, *Joseph: God Planned it for Good* (Lincoln, NE: Back to the Bible Publications, 1971) 7.

God's forgiveness and favor rested upon Joseph. Such forgiveness and favor would not have happened without such confession and repentance.

Joseph has now learned plenty in order to teach a pagan culture something about which it currently knows nothing. As Joseph emerges and becomes the Prime Minister of Egypt, we should take note that he is in a place not only to *be* the Prime Minister, but *to minister.* He will administrate, organize, rally and stockpile. He will display business qualities and economic skills that would make Wall Street stop. His plans of storing and preserving are something straight out of some of the best university economics classes – even of this day. But most importantly, he will teach a pagan nation about love and forgiveness. How difficult will that be? Telfer describes how foreign such an idea may have appeared to them:

> Religion creates a sense of personal relation with deity. In the pagan religions which surrounded, first Israel, and then the Christian Church, there was hope of the favor of the gods and fear of offending them, but no thought of their forgiving offences. Forgiveness appeared to be a change of mind, and it would seem beneath the dignity of deity to undergo a change of mind towards mortals. In the god of Greek philosophers, on the other hand, such an idea as divine forgiveness would be unthinkable, since immutability appeared to be a necessary attribute of deity. [38]

Maybe on simple, human levels, some Egyptians could understand a measure of love, caring, compassion and forgiveness among family members, loved ones and friends, but Joseph's place of preparation has revealed to him a concept unlike anything known heretofore or thereafter: true forgiveness. Only when Jesus arrived and walked on this earth was this idea more fully demonstrated. Whatever Joseph learned, he learned it well. He followed the compass closely, and Joseph *"... went through all the land of Egypt"* (Genesis 41:46b NASB). He most assuredly had "the freedom of the seas."

---

38   W. Telfer, *The Forgiveness of Sins: An Essay in the History of Christian Doctrine and Practice* (Philadelphia, PA: Muhlenberg Press, 1959) 15.

MASTERING QUALITIES BEFORE SPEAKING GOD'S TRUTH

Have you ever heard that old adage, "Nice guys finish last?" That seems to be the prevailing secular thinking today. It is a worldly and false concept, clearly refuted in many parts of Scripture, and decisively shattered in the example and character of Joseph. Many truths are learned from Joseph's emergence, but I will share three basic thoughts that help us embrace forgiveness and exemplify a forgiving spirit.

I. HUMILITY AND A GENTLE SPIRIT PAVE THE WAY FOR THE BELIEVER TO SPEAK GOD'S TRUTH.

We shared earlier that there is a genuineness in Joseph. Very likely, that is the reason Joseph now has Pharaoh's ear. Joseph explains a real truth when he says, *"... God has revealed to Pharaoh what He is about to do"* (Genesis 41:25). Earlier, Joseph explains this clearly: *"I cannot do it," Joseph replied to Pharaoh, "but God will give Pharaoh the answer he desires"* (Genesis 41:16b).

The work done in Joseph's heart has been genuine and complete, testifying to God's miraculous handiwork in this man's life. Have you noticed that such evidence was not present when Joseph was thrown into the pit by his brothers? We see the new Joseph now. Therefore, what else could be Joseph's conclusion but that none of it was about him? It was about what God wanted to relate to Pharaoh and wanted to do for His people. I like how the King James Bible puts it: *"And Joseph answered Pharaoh, saying, 'It is not in me: God shall give Pharaoh an answer of peace'"* (Genesis 41:16 KJV).

You and I can be certain that when the interpretation of Pharaoh's dream was revealed and announced, every demon in Hell must have screamed. Now they realized that redemption was on the way and there was no chance of stopping its arrival. Joseph was genuinely humble, embracing forgiveness and exhibiting a redemptive character, which is imperative for all who call themselves by the Name of Christ.

II. CONFESSION, REPENTANCE, AND SEEKING FORGIVENESS ARE PARAMOUNT PRIOR TO SPEAKING GOD'S TRUTH.

The Church used to speak a great deal about this. Today, much of that teaching and preaching has been abandoned in favor of more "felt-need" preaching. Even back as far as 1970, Alvin Rogness recognized this sad trend. Listen to these words, and you decide: Are they relevant today?

It is one of the strange phenomena of our time that just at the moment in history when the secular world, through its writers of fiction, its dramatists, and it psychiatrists, speaks more universally of the sense of guilt than ever before – that just at this moment the church speaks less of confession and forgiveness than ever before.[39]

You would think Rogness was speaking those words about our time. That was written in 1970. Can our heart ever be ready to experience the healing it needs without first seeking God's forgiveness? Can our mouth ever be truly prepared to speak God's truth without first confessing? Can an author write about real love without first experiencing the love of God? God has a true, forgiving heart, and without communing with the heart of the heavenly Father – without chasing after His heart – we can never genuinely know the expanse and the depth of what real forgiveness entails.

As the story progresses, we will see that Joseph arrives at a place where he is able not only to embrace forgiveness, but to extend it wherever it is needed at any time. Such a heart attitude was not preceded by an easy journey, and Joseph is still not aware that he will be called on to test this inner attitude of forgiveness.

How interesting life can be when it teaches us things about patience, forgiveness and a compassionate heart; we never really know what level we have reached until the opportunity arises for us to extend those qualities. Embracing and extending forgiveness is a long process, and it can be argued that often the child of God rushes the process, paroling himself on an early release program from his prison cell so that he may be thrust back into the mainstream of society as quickly as possible. However,

---

39   Alvin Rogness, *Forgiveness and Confession* (Minneapolis, MN: Augsburg Publishing House, 1970) 51.

if we balk at the process, the potential arises for more, not less, bitterness, resentment and anger to erupt. We *must* work through the process of forgiveness – every part of it – and not try to escape it, or healing will inevitably be delayed, as George Lawson explains:

> We are too ready in word and in tongue to forgive those who have offended us, whilst in deed and in truth we retain a bitter resentment of our wrongs; and if we do not inflict or wish some visible judgment to come on them, we wish that they may feel in their own heart a painful remembrance of what they have done. But Joseph so entirely forgave his sinning brethren, that he wished for them the same peace and pleasure that he wished for himself. [40]

In other words, there must be a complete follow-through, and in order to get from the "now" to the "not-yet," we must *press hard into* the Father and work through the process. The road to forgiving others runs right through the middle of the towns of confession, repentance and asking for God's forgiveness in the life of the one who must extend that forgiveness to the offender. That is where it starts, and there is no detour. It is a road less traveled, but it is a road that *must* be traveled.

III. DILIGENCE AND ATTENTION TO DETAIL IS ESSENTIAL IN SPEAKING GOD'S TRUTH.

As Joseph relates the interpretation of the dreams to Pharaoh, then gives the prognosis of the situation, we could almost assume that Joseph had been preparing for such a speech for months, as one would prepare for an exam. On the contrary, no such indication is given in Scripture, and it is more likely that Joseph gave the blueprint for the nation's success verbatim as God revealed the plan on the spot.

Whether you prepare for months, years, or decades – or minutes; whether you use notes or go empty handed; whether you speak extemporaneously or use a prepared speech, attention to detail *must* be adhered to explicitly. Joseph's ability to accomplish such a feat reveals his

---

40   George Lawson, *Lectures on the History of Joseph* (Chatham, England: W & J
       Mackay Limited, 1807) 266.

pure heart and motive, and he demonstrates that he has been a man who has not ventured far from the presence of the Lord.

Spending great lengths of time in the prayer closet is good for the child of God, but on those occasions when time is of the essence and there is little or no time for preparation, the believer must always claim the promise found in James; *"If any of you lacks wisdom, you should ask God, who gives generously to all without finding fault, and it will be given to you"* (James 1:5). Even a prayer under the breath saying, "God, as I go into this situation, grant me your wisdom. I didn't know this situation was going to come up and it caught me off guard. I'm walking into an impromptu meeting, but I believe that this didn't catch you off guard. Lord, I need wisdom and I need it five minutes from now. God, this is a *James 1:5 moment*. Please grant me wisdom very quickly." Even a prayer like that is better than blindly walking into a circumstance with a ton of notes and going in all alone. God is always faithful to a pure heart and a right motive. He will give you wisdom, and onlookers will observe the God who is resident within your being. God will provide you what is needed at the time it is needed if you will acknowledge His presence and power. God will give spiritual satisfaction, as Watchman Nee describes:

> God never sells anything. "Gift" means something freely given. God always gives freely to men. And He will give to whoever asks. God gives us sunlight without charge; He gives us rainfall without cost. He will also give you spiritual satisfaction in exactly the same fashion.[41]

When it comes time to relate God's truth, we should be as precise as Joseph was and listen to that still, small voice that is trying to speak to us. Pay attention to detail. Whether the topic is finances, theology or relating God's truth to children, He is certain to provide wisdom to you. And since the promise of God is real and He is going to answer the prayer for wisdom, pay attention to it and watch for the details. Then stand back and be amazed: Here comes the wisdom! In the final analysis, make sure

---

41 Watchman Nee, *Full of Grace and Truth, Vol. 2* (New York, NY: Christian Fellowship Publishers, Inc., 1981) 54.

God gets the credit and any glory. Never take credit for God's wisdom that is granted to you. When God gives it, it is really His wisdom to you on loan. Give Him the credit and the glory.

Here is another thing to consider: We must always stand guard and be ready to execute the very truth God is giving us. Once Joseph had told Pharaoh what needed to happen in order to keep the nation from starving, Pharaoh essentially said, "You are my distinguished financier. You are hired! Go and do it" (paraphrased). Furthermore, Pharaoh said, *"... 'I am Pharaoh, but without your word no one will lift hand or foot in all Egypt'"* (Genesis 41:44b). If God reveals it to you, be ready to actually do it.

Have you ever experienced a time when you had a great idea and everyone else thought it was terrific too, but no one wanted to carry it out? It is not uncommon that when the Christian obtains the wisdom that he or she seeks from the Lord and relates His plan, those outside the plan and/ or outside the will of God who nonetheless support the plan, they often immediately enlist the expositor (the one who came up with the idea) to administrate it.

I heard about a boss who told his employee, "That's a great idea! You may initiate your idea and do anything here you want ... so long as you do it!" If God gives you the plan, be aware that you may be called upon to facilitate that plan. But think of it: Who better to facilitate the plan than the one who is holding onto and living by the compass? That one is now at the helm and has the freedom of the seas.

CHAPTER SIX

JOSEPH'S DEFINING MOMENTS IN DISPLAYING FORGIVENESS

Since 1811, the United States government has kept records of people sending in anonymous letters with money in the envelopes. People have long been known to do this because they have felt guilty about cheating the government out of money. Some might have cheated on their taxes, stolen public property or something from a national park, etc. Later, feeling guilty about their crime, they decide to pay the money back. I read a story in a local newspaper about one such letter written to the government from a person who allegedly cheated the Internal Revenue Service. The letter read, "Here is the money I cheated the government out of last year, and if I still cannot go to sleep, I'll send you the rest." There was $1,000 in cash enclosed in the envelope.

The human conscience is an amazing gift from God. However, if a person habitually sins and keeps telling himself that his behavior is okay, his conscience is blunted and ultimately destroyed. The person becomes numb to the destructive power of sin, damaging his ability to have a healthy outlook on life and a healthy self-image.

Events in chapter 42 of Genesis take place approximately twenty years after events in chapter 37 when Joseph was sold by his brothers into slavery. What has happened to Jacob's sons back in Canaan? Have they gone on with their lives and forgotten about Joseph? Or will their father say something to them that will trigger their hardened consciences, their covered-up guilt, and their old grudge against a barely-remembered sibling? No one in the family has seen or heard from Joseph in twenty years or more, which makes Genesis 42 a fascinating chapter.

Have you ever thought to yourself, "I have forgiven the one who hurt me ... or at least I think I have. How do I really know if I have?" In

the

following paragraphs, we will look at three major aspects of embracing forgiveness; occurrences that inevitably precede the extending of true forgiveness. Then we will consider a fourth aspect of our experiences that enables us to reach a point of forgiveness. These elements of forgiveness will assist you and me to know whether or not we have truly forgiven the one who hurt us:

I. GOD WILL ALLOW YOU AND ME TO EXPERIENCE A RANGE OF CIRCUMSTANCES IN ORDER TO SOFTEN A HARDENED CONSCIENCE.

Chapter 42 of Genesis brings us back to the land of Canaan. The scene has shifted, and we are "back at the ranch" in Jacob's tents. As the famine intensifies, Jacob discovers that there is grain in Egypt and says to his sons in the first verse, *"...Why do you just keep looking at each other?"* (Genesis 42:1b).

I have read that a bunch of times, and I have often felt that if this were not such a serious situation, that statement would be quite humorous. It is reminiscent of my dad telling my brothers and me about a particular Saturday morning chore he wanted us to do, when, after five minutes of no action, he might say, "Why are you boys just standing around doing nothing? I've told you what to do, now get to work!" I almost have to chuckle at that phrase because I can visualize it so well in my own dad. Jacob wanted those boys to go down to Egypt and buy some grain, and they're just standing around looking at each other. Jacob wants action!

The lean years that Joseph told Pharaoh about are now in full swing. The seven years of plenty are over, and the country is in the grip of famine, a famine so severe that it extends beyond the borders of Egypt. Canaan is affected. Jacob is essentially saying to his sons, "Look guys, if we are going to survive this, you boys are going to have to stop standing around here staring at each other. Get down to Egypt and buy us some grain!" (paraphrased).

I'm just speculating here, but could it be that for a brief moment those ten boys had exactly the same thought: "Wait a minute: When we sold Joseph, wasn't he headed for Egypt?" Can you picture their unease?

See their eyes shifting back and forth! Maybe for the first time in a long time they are thinking about Joseph. Whatever the case, God will now take them through circumstances that will wake up their unconscious consciences; how God does that will become very clear.

II. THERE ARE TIMES WHEN GOD ALLOWS US TO EXPERIENCE UNPRECEDENTED BLESSINGS IN ORDER TO SPEAK TO OUR HARDENED CONSCIENCE.

These ten brothers had twenty years where their flocks and herds had multiplied, where they had made money, where they had prospered and where God had watched over every part of their wealth. They had practically become sheiks, to use Middle Eastern terminology. God had incredibly blessed them in spite of what they had done.

But you may remember that this also happened to someone else in Scripture. Let's take a brief field trip, a side excursion for just a moment, to another part of the Old Testament; to Hosea and his wife, Gomer. You may recall that the prophet Hosea married a woman who was a prostitute because God told him to marry her. She remained unfaithful to Hosea, and in fact, she eventually left him and went off to have one affair after another. All the time she was having these affairs, Hosea took care of her. In telling the story, Hosea says, *"For she does not know that it was I who gave her the grain, the new wine and the oil, and lavished on her silver and gold, which they used for Baal"* (Hosea 2:8 NASB).

The entire time Gomer was having these relationships, Hosea was sending her bread, water, wool, flax, oil, money and everything she needed. He blessed her and took care of her in the midst of and despite her sin.

In the same way, the ten brothers of Joseph were blessed by God for approximately twenty years despite their sin and guilt. That sort of thing happens throughout Scripture, and it is nothing less than the grace, the goodness and the compassion of God, who is saying, "I am going to bless you, even in the midst of your sin, because I want to reach that conscience of yours!" This is what the Apostle Paul is alluding to in Romans when he says, *"Or do you show contempt for the riches of his kindness, forbearance and patience, not realizing that God's kindness is intended to lead you to repentance?"* (Romans 2:4).

When we have unconfessed sin in our life, it may not be apparent that God has blessed us financially, materially or intellectually, and Paul is saying, "Don't you realize that this is God trying to speak to your conscience?" (paraphrased). Every blessing that comes to the believer in the midst of sin is God telling us to wake up before judgment comes.

God is good, and He heaps blessing upon blessing when we do not deserve it. That is because He is trying to alert an unconscious conscience. If blessings do not get our attention, then buffeting may; God will use both circumstances to reach us.

III. WHEN BLESSINGS WILL NOT GET OUR ATTENTION, GOD MAY ALLOW CRISIS INTO OUR LIVES.

That is what happened to Gomer. God speaks through Hosea and says, *"Therefore, I will take back My grain at harvest time and My new wine in its season. I will also take away My wool and My flax given to cover her nakedness. And then I will uncover her lewdness in the sight of her lovers, and no one will rescue her out of My hand"* (Hosea 2:9–10 NASB).

The story of Hosea and Gomer, incidentally, parallels God's relationship to the Hebrew nation and the Church. Hosea represents God and Gomer represents God's people (Israel and also the Church) who turn away from the Lord. It is a picture of how God came to His own but His own would not receive Him. As a result of Gomer's refusal to respond to blessing, God removes that blessing. Returning to Genesis 42, we read that the ten brothers receive the order from their father to go down to Egypt and seek grain. You have to wonder if their past actions come flooding back to their minds: "I can't believe it!" They may be thinking, "We're headed for the very place where we sent Joseph."

Of course, if the boys did think this, they might also have added, "But Egypt is so huge, with such a large population, and Joseph is probably not even alive anymore. There is no way he could have survived a life of slavery in that country. Even if he did, it is highly unlikely we will run into him." At any rate, I can assure you that they are now facing their guilt. How do I know? We will address that a little later, but these ten brothers are definitely having to wake up and acknowledge what they did so many years ago.

These sorts of things happen all the time in life; God will allow us to go through some crisis, some emergency, or some tragedy to get the conscience to become conscious. Sometimes He reaches us through blessings; at other times, through crisis, and in both cases the purpose of the Lord is to awaken us from our slumber and break through to our blunted conscience.

There is a fourth way that God may bring us to a point where we are better able to ask forgiveness and to forgive:

IV. SOMETIMES, GOD ALLOWS US TO ENDURE THE TREATMENT THAT WE HAVE METED OUT TO OTHERS.

Did you ever stop to think that God may allow us to endure the very thing, in the very same way, that we have done to someone else in order to uncover our hidden guilt? This is what happens to Joseph's brothers.

The ten men arrive in Egypt, and we have a description of their meeting with Joseph:

"Now Joseph was the governor of the land, the person who sold grain to all its people. So when Joseph's brothers arrived, they bowed down to him with their faces to the ground. As soon as Joseph saw his brothers, he recognized them, but he pretended to be a stranger and spoke harshly to them. 'Where do you come from?' he asked.

"'From the land of Canaan,' they replied, 'to buy food.'

"Although Joseph recognized his brothers, they did not recognize him. Then he remembered his dreams about them and said to them, 'You are spies! You have come to see where our land is unprotected.'" (Genesis 42:6-9).

When approaching this part of the story, often people think that Joseph is not acting with integrity; that perhaps he is acting out of anger or a grudge and seeks to pay back his brothers. I have taught and preached on this passage many times; without fail, I am approached later by someone saying that I favored Joseph way too much, that Joseph was too harsh with his brothers and was acting in revenge. Although that may appear to be the case at first glance, I am convinced that a careful examination of the facts will prove otherwise.

First of all as I stated earlier, these brothers were cruel and hardened men. I am sure that they had iced water flowing through their veins. There is Reuben, who committed incest with his father's concubine. (His father should not have had concubines in the first place, but that is another discussion about dysfunction for another time.) There is Judah, who committed incest with his daughter-in-law. Then there are Simeon and Levi, who acted like terrorists, going into Shechem and butchering everyone. This is a dysfunctional family with such a past that even Hollywood could not have made it up. They talked about murdering their brother, and only abstained because he was worth more to them if sold.

Joseph is not ungodly, and in speaking this way to them, he may have been, for a few moments, in self-protection mode. He has not seen them in over twenty years; how does he know that they are indeed not spies or seeking to exploit and hurt him once again? What confirmation does he have? They explain why they are there, but how does Joseph know that this is the truth? They treated him badly twenty years ago, and Joseph has no way of knowing if they have become worse since he knew them. He must be careful.

Scholars disagree as to whether or not Joseph's brothers had repented by the time they stood in front of him. Had they reformed, or not? Nahum Sarna seems to indicate that they might have repented:

> The main interest of the narrative is now in the complex human situation, the fulfillment in the life of Joseph's boyhood dreams, the interplay of emotions, the testing of the brothers' honesty and sense of fraternal love and responsibility. Joseph forces his brothers into a position in which they have no option but to appear once again before him together with his own dear Benjamin. The climax of the drama is at hand. Joseph carefully contrives a desperate situation

in which the brothers are compelled to show, once and for all, whether they have reformed since the day they so brutally sold him into slavery. [42]

On the other hand, Keil and Delitzsch seem to imply the brothers had not yet fully repented:

And with his harsh mode of addressing them, Joseph had no intention whatever to administer to his brethren a just punishment for their wickedness towards him, for his heart could not have stooped to such mean revenge; but he wanted to probe thoroughly the feelings of their hearts, whether they felt that they deserved the punishment of God for the sin they committed, and how they felt towards their aged father and their youngest brother. Even in the fact that he did not send the one away directly to fetch Benjamin, and merely detain the rest, but put the whole ten in prison, and afterwards modify his threat, there was no indecision as to the manner in which he should behave towards them – no wavering between thoughts of wrath and revenge on the one hand, and forgiving love and meekness on the other; but he hoped by imprisoning them to make his brethren feel the earnestness of his words, and to give them time for reflection, as the curt "is no more" with which they had alluded to Joseph's removal was a sufficient proof that they had not yet truly repented of the deed. [43]

Still another author, William Taylor, has no doubt. He is quite convinced that the brothers have fully repented:

He saw that they had fully repented of their sin against him, and therefore, when he observed that they were troubled at his presence, he said to them, "Be not grieved, nor angry with yourselves..." Had they not been really penitent it might have been dangerous to preach such doctrine to them. But they had come to hate their sin, and were now in such a state of mind regarding it as to be

42   Nahum M. Sarna, *Understanding Genesis: The Heritage of Biblical Israel* (New York, NY: McGraw-Hill Book Company, 1966) 223.

43   C.F. Keil and F. Delitzsch, *Commentary on the Old Testament in Ten Volumes, Vol. 1* (Grand Rapids, MI: Eerdmans Publishing Company, reprinted 1985) 355-356.

verging towards despair, so that they required to be encouraged and comforted. And nothing could have been better calculated to lift them out of their despondency than the presentation of this aspect of divine providence. [44]

I am of the opinion that the boys had not fully repented, although I admit that I cannot fully substantiate that belief. It will forever remain speculation. My opinion is such because after Jacob died, according to Genesis 50:15–21, the boys still lived in fear and needed to be convinced of Joseph's love and forgiveness toward them. In addition, it seems that the brothers later resort to telling a lie or a half-truth; again, something I cannot prove. Yet it seems likely to me that in this latter incident, they are not entirely honest and therefore not entirely repentant. A careful examination of Genesis 50:15–21 will reveal why I say this, but we will get to that a little later.

It is, however, a good thing to look at the state of these boys' hearts to understand what Joseph was facing. Joseph has no clue why they are really there; if he does believe they are coming to buy grain, no doubt he wonders what else they have up their sleeves. Scripture substantiates that they were there to buy grain; we know that from Jacob's words, but Joseph does not know that. But have they *genuinely repented* or have they not? If not, they may yet be a danger to Joseph; if they have, it would not be obvious to Joseph at this time.

The casual onlooker who thinks that Joseph is just being a bully may also fail to appreciate the extent of the traumas he has been through. They have no doubt shaped his initial reaction. Although it has not been defined as such until modern times, Joseph may in fact have experienced post-traumatic stress syndrome. Athalya Brenner, Archie Chi-Chung Lee and Gale Yee discuss this syndrome in relation to Joseph. One of the authors (it is not made clear which one) reflects on the value of Joseph's story for our own healing:

---

44   William M. Taylor, *Joseph: The Prime Minister* (Grand Rapids, MI: Baker Book House, 1961) 137.

In contemplating this theme, I felt for a time I was sublimating my own sense of personal trauma: inasmuch as engaging in biblical literature is a form of sublimation, the process was partially therapeutic. The sublime nature of this particular biblical story [Joseph] (which undoubtedly nurtures its religious meanings) is connected, I believe, with its telling and showing of a traumatic and therapeutic process.

Joseph "remembered the dreams," not just any dreams but, as the narrative stresses, those "which he had dreamt about them," about his brothers (Genesis 42:9). This moment of recollection is described in the sequence of Joseph's estranged encounter with his brothers as a flicker of consciousness. The content of the dreams, which he had dreamed a long time before, is not conveyed or retold by the narrator, for in identifying with the stirring of Joseph's memory, the reader is also to awaken in himself or herself some recollection of these dreams however flimsy, registering them, for a passing moment: the first dreams, about the brothers' sheaves; gathering round in the field and bowing down before Joseph's upright sheaf, and the second dream, about the sun and the moon and the eleven stars bowing down to him (Genesis 37:5-11).

Joseph's indistinct reminiscence of the dreams is in tune with the terseness of biblical narrative art and with the elusiveness of memory as a psychic phenomenon. However, "other" dreams, namely nightmares of remembered or unremembered horrors Joseph may have dreamt "about them," his brothers, in the twenty years that have lapsed since their last fatal encounter, also are evoked by the particular wording and the immediate and wider narrative context of the phrase, "And Joseph remembered the dreams he dreamt for them" (a verbatim translation of 42:9). As if behind the memory of the symbolic dreams, there lurks another memory, unstated, that of a traumatic event, which tends to surface in the dreams, of what occurred to Joseph when his brothers had come close to his attempted murder by throwing him, after stripping him of his exceptional garment, presumably close to naked, into a pit, later selling him off to merchant travelers who happened to pass by, brutally severing him from his protective father and destining him to what in all likelihood can be imagined as a life of slavery and exile. Surely, in paraphrasing Shakespeare's *Tempest,* "such stuff" are nightmares made of. [45]

I found this to be an interesting excerpt in that it shows how, by assimilating Joseph's story at a deeper level than merely intellectual, his healing process can be made a part of our own.

Given the extent of the trauma, Joseph may well have reacted in something of a self-preservation mode. It could be that Joseph really does not know why the brothers have come and needs to test them and see for himself if they are sincere; once convinced of their sincerity, he may well intend good for these brothers.

Joseph has always been a man of God. In making a character assessment, Brenner, Lee and Yee provide another interesting observation: "... these desperate characters are a threesome: Joseph, his brothers, and Jacob, all locked in a posttraumatic triangle, out of which only Joseph is strong enough to fully emerge." [46]

Joseph was a man of God in his father's house, in Potiphar's house, in jail, and now in Pharaoh's palace – even royalty has not changed him one bit, and if he has been changed, it has only been for the good. Therefore, Joseph is not acting in an ungodly way. On the contrary, he is doing exactly what God is leading him to do. God desires a relationship with these boys, and Joseph will desire that too as will soon be evident.

So why didn't Joseph just come out with it? "Hey guys, it's me! Your brother, Joseph! Remember me?" Not only will Joseph not do that, but he will take great pains to cover up who he is. Notice again in verse 7, where it says, according to the *NASB, "When Joseph saw his brothers he recognized*

---

45   Athalya Brenner, Archie Chi-Chung Lee, and Gale A. Yee, editors, *Genesis* (Minneapolis, MN: Fortress Press, 2010) 149-150.

46   Ibid., 148.

them, but he disguised himself to them and spoke to them harshly. And he said to them, 'Where have you come from?'" (Genesis 42:7 NASB). Other translations say that he made himself strange to them.

How does Joseph disguise himself? He disguises himself by speaking harshly to them. That fact is enough to speak of his character, and this one verse could provide the basis for an entire sermon on the character of a man. Joseph knew that if he spoke to them in the way he normally spoke to people, they would know immediately who he was. These brothers had so intimidated him in those early years that they would not see the hand of God in all of this but may try to use him for what they could get. He knew that if he spoke harshly to them, his identity would remain hidden because harshness was quite out of character for him. The other way he disguised himself was by using an interpreter. He had no need of one, and probably even the interpreter knew that. Consequently, the interpreter plays along. But this enhances his disguise to the brothers.

Another thing that we might miss in a shallow reading of the piece is that if Joseph had his way, it is possible that he would have revealed himself to his brothers. But God is so much in this – God is so much all over Joseph in this moment that Joseph has almost become another man – a godly man. He appears to be restrained by God. And the reason is that God has a greater purpose; the salvation of Joseph's brothers. You and I need to understand that God will allow us to endure the treatment that we have given out to others in order to uncover some hidden sin or long-suppressed guilt in our life. So Joseph covers up who he is and allows his brothers to experience the two things they put Joseph through. What were these?

Joseph accuses the brothers of being spies; that is something they accused Joseph of back in Dothan. Here, Joseph accuses them of being spies, but the brothers deny Joseph's accusation and claim to be honest and true men, which is rather humorous in itself.

Do you recall Genesis 37, when Joseph went to check on his brothers and found them in Dothan? He was sent there by his father to check on them, not to spy on them. They accused him of spying to gather information in order to report back to Jacob. Maybe they suspected that because earlier in chapter 37, that is exactly what Joseph had done. In their eyes, Joseph is a spy, so when Joseph comes to Dothan, they accuse him of this very thing.

Fast forward to Egypt and Genesis 42:13 where the brothers say, "...*Thy servants are twelve brethren, the sons of one man in the land of Canaan; and, behold, the youngest is this day with our father,* **and one is not**" (Genesis 42:13 *KJV*, bold, mine). It makes me wonder if Joseph in his flesh was thinking to himself, "One is not? Oh buddy, you do not know what you're saying. You are clueless, and you're about to find out differently." The *NASB* indicates that the brothers said, "*... and one is no longer alive.*" [47] Seemingly, the guilt in them is beginning to be unearthed. It is an amazing fact that when we are treated in the same way as we have treated others, the sense of guilt begins to surface. So the first thing Joseph does to these brothers is to accuse them of being spies just as they accused him.

In addition, Joseph throws the brothers into a prison; that is something they did to Joseph. Genesis 42:17 of the *King James Version* calls it a ward, but Joseph essentially puts them in prison, or in a place of holding. It would be interesting to know what they talked about while in that holding cell. All ten of them are in prison together, and while in prison they do think and talk about Joseph, as the text bears out: "*They said to one another, 'Surely we are being punished because of our brother. We saw how distressed he was when he pleaded with us for his life, but we would not listen; that's why this distress has come on us'*" (Genesis 42:21). My first response to this verse is, "Ya think, guys?" And yet some still think that Joseph is being a bully. No, what you see here is a process that I believe is not directed by Joseph, but by God. What we do not see at first is that the process is building up to Joseph's eventual embracing of forgiveness.

My sense is that these men have had a hardened conscience for the last twenty years, and that when their dad tells them to go to Egypt, something stirs within them. It appears that they are being prepared; their hearts are being slightly unraveled so that they may perhaps understand the

---

47   Genesis 42:13b *The Holy Bible, New American Standard Bible* (Grand Rapids, MI: Zondervan, 1999).

forgiveness extended to them. Certainly they are at a place where their hard consciences are laid bare and softened. They are now discussing things that they have not discussed in years. Perhaps they sense a change coming; one can imagine that it is a puzzling and stirring time for them.

The amazing thing to me is that Joseph is going to extend full forgiveness to these guys. This grabs my attention and I want to say to Joseph, "How is this possible after what they did to you?" There is no portrayal of forgiveness at this magnitude anywhere else in the Old Testament. Jesus has not yet walked on this earth. Calvary has not yet happened. So how does Joseph know how to forgive at such depth, especially when the brothers have shown no signs of repentance? Reuben is still not repentant. Reuben is still trying to make himself look good in verse 22: *"Reuben replied, 'Didn't I tell you not to sin against the boy? But you wouldn't listen! Now we must give an accounting for his blood'"* (Genesis 42:22).

Something is beginning to stir in these boys, but Reuben is not there yet and is still at the stage of, "I told you so." Yet Reuben is just as much a part of this sin as are the others. Being the oldest, he could have been a good influence on the others, and he would have revealed genuine repentance if he had said something like, "You are right, and we should repent immediately." Reuben was an accomplice in this because it was Reuben who suggested throwing Joseph into the pit back in chapter 37. He could have stopped it. Furthermore, instead of keeping their act a secret for twenty years, he could have told their father the truth. Reuben could have encouraged repentance immediately, and now Reuben is trying to take credit for saying, "I told you we shouldn't have done this."

If only we Christians could remember to run hard and fast to the Lord with repentance, then we would find complete forgiveness just as quickly as Joseph's brothers are going to receive it from Joseph. What Reuben needs to do is stop pointing the figure and praising his own efforts, and along with the others, repent of everything and come clean, as Solomon Schechter points out:

> Thus neither the quantity of sins, nor the quality of sins, need make man hesitate to follow the Divine call to repentance. He has only

to approach, so to speak, the "door" with the determination of repentance, and it will be widely opened for his admittance as it was for Joseph and his brothers.[48]

Do you see why Reuben, even though he is the oldest, cannot lead this family? They all confess, but Reuben still has a ways to go. Nevertheless, all ten of them sense that their past actions are coming home to roost, and they are going through a necessary process of facing their own guilt.

The text records Reuben as saying in verse 22, "... *Now we must give an accounting for his blood*" (Genesis 42:22b). What Reuben is essentially saying is that there is a reckoning approaching and a record kept against them. He is correct, and it is God who is keeping the record.

Verse 23 verifies that Joseph understood all that the brothers were saying, and that the interpreter before them was only a prop. Joseph has not said anything to them yet about what they did, but he is a smart man. He is very well aware that God is causing them to understand that they are being punished for all they did. It is all coming to the surface as they confess to one another, not realizing that they are exposing their feelings of guilt to Joseph, who furthermore, understands every word.

When we are treated the same way we have treated others, it may take a while to dawn on us, but eventually we discover how wrong we were to do what we did. That hardened conscience softens, and that hidden guilt moves to the surface.

RECIPIENTS OF HIS GRACE

Is it possible that at this point Joseph is still holding a grudge? There are some wonderful Christian scholars who say yes he is, but I say absolutely not. A careful examination of Genesis 41:50–52 reveals that God has blessed Joseph and been gracious to him. We discover in those verses that God has given him sons; "Manasseh," which means or is derived from "forget" because, as Joseph says, God made him forget all of his trouble, and "Ephraim," which sounds like the Hebrew word for "twice fruitful" because, as Joseph says, God made him fruitful in the land of his troubles

---

48   Solomon Schechter, *Some Aspects of Rabbinic Theology* (New York, NY: The Macmillan Company, 1923) 326-327.

and affliction. There is no chance, in my opinion, that Joseph is holding a grudge.

Joseph is dealing with these brothers because he has a heart to see them come to know God. He wants the relationship restored, but more than that, it is obvious he wants them to know God the way he knows God. He has no intention of retaliation. He executes whatever judgment God orders him to mete out, and no more. The purpose of the judgment is not revenge. It is for God to break the will, heart and spirit of these brothers, and bring them to repentance.

Whatever else Joseph is experiencing in his heart right now, he is aware that something supernatural is taking place. Helmut Thielicke, quoting Ralf Luther, said something interesting about seeing things that are supernatural in others, in his book, *Life Can Begin Again,* in a chapter entitled, "No Retaliation":

> Ralf Luther once expressed it this way: "To love one's enemy does not mean to love the mire in which the pearl lies, but to love the pearl that lies in the mire." So love for one's enemy is not based on an act of will, a kind of 'self-control' by which I try to suppress all feelings of hatred (this would lead only to complexes and false and forced actions), but rather upon a gift, a gift of grace that gives me new eyes, so that with these new eyes I can see something divine in others. [49]

Joseph knows God is up to something unique. He now decides to let them go back home, but there is a stipulation; he needs proof that they are not spies. He instructs them to go back to Canaan and fetch their younger brother Benjamin, while he holds Simeon for ransom.

Lest you think that Joseph is not tender toward his brothers, you need only read the twenty-fourth verse; *"He turned away from them and began to weep, but then came back and spoke to them again ..."* (Genesis 42:24a). This is the tenderness of Joseph's heart. This is the love that he has for them; there is no grudge in him. There is an uncontrollable weeping. He is sobbing, and it makes me wonder as he wept, what he may have been

---

49   Helmut Thielicke, *Life Can Begin Again* (Philadelphia, PA: Fortress Press, 1963) 75.

saying under his breath; perhaps, "God, I do not want to do it this way," but he seemingly has a mandate from God. No doubt, he is brokenhearted over the lost condition of his brothers, but he has his orders. Nicoll and Van Dyke are rather impressed with Joseph's way of handling this situation:

We cannot but admire the conduct of Joseph in this remarkable interview. He had learned to look at his whole life in the light of God's Providence, and in his resignation to that he found it easy to forgive his brethren. "Ye thought evil against me: but God meant it unto good."

Here is the "open secret" of that marvelous equanimity which is so characteristic of his demeanor. He traced God's hand in every incident of his history. He accepted the lot which God assigned him, and wherever he was he had the unfaltering conviction that "God meant it unto good." If we had the same trust in the wise and loving arrangements of an all-superintending God, we, too, might continue peaceful amid all the changes and surprises of our unsettled and fleeting lives.[50]

Joseph commands that the brothers' sacks be filled with corn and that their money be restored to them so as to give them provisions for the journey back to Canaan. Yet when one of them opens his sack to feed his donkey, he notices that the money they had intended to use in payment for the grain is still there. Verse 28 says, *"'My silver has been returned,' he said to his brothers. 'Here it is in my sack.' Their hearts sank and they turned to each other trembling and said, 'What is this that God has done to us?'"* (Genesis 42:28).

Be assured, Joseph is not holding a grudge. He is assisting the Lord in bringing them to an understanding of who is really in charge. Their hearts sink in verse 28, for now these boys know (and have proclaimed out loud) that God is up to something. This is not Joseph's doing, and they are not standing before a ruler any more. They have just had God intervene in their lives. This money in their bags is no accident, and they know it. Maybe if

---

50   W. Robertson Nicoll and H.J. Van Dyke, *139 Sermon Outlines on the Old Testament* (Grand Rapids, MI: Baker Book House, 1957) 22.

only one had found his money put back in his bag, they may have assumed a mistake had been made. But when they see that the money is back in every bag, they know God is involved.

Jacob's sons finally understand that they have not received justice, but grace. They are loaded down with grace. Consequently, one of the brothers says, *"... What is this that God has done to us?"* (Genesis 42:28b).

Did you notice that this is the first time in the entire story that one of those ten brothers uses the name of God? They have never spoken about God before. Joseph has. Over and over again Joseph has talked about God, but not one of those ten brothers ever mentions the holy name of God. Now they know that *Elohim* is doing something in their lives, that they have been recipients of grace, and finally Reuben will start to take responsibility as we see in Genesis 42:37. Furthermore in Chapter 43, Judah also takes responsibility before Jacob for protecting Benjamin on the journey back to Egypt.

Someone once defined the concepts of justice, mercy and grace in this manner: Justice is getting what you deserve; mercy is not getting what you deserve; grace is getting what you do not deserve. And *forgiveness embraced* makes grace possible. Grace, when we sense it and respond to it, works wonders in the lives of human beings. What Joseph's brothers deserved was justice. Instead, they found mercy, and they received grace. Furthermore, they could never have dreamed in their wildest imagination that forgiveness to this extent would be embraced and extended.

MARKERS OF FORGIVENESS

The story continues as the brothers return to Canaan, spend just long enough there to consume all the grain, and then return to Egypt, this time with Benjamin, their younger brother. Once again, they present themselves at the palace and find themselves back in "interview mode" before Joseph.

Throughout our study, it has been said that embracing forgiveness is a process. Have you ever thought to yourself, "How can I know if I have completely forgiven my offender? I want to forgive, but how sure can I be that I really *have* forgiven?" In other cases someone might say, "Should I even forgive since my offender has not asked for forgiveness?" The latter will be answered before the former because it is vitally important that we understand that forgiveness is to be extended whether the offender has asked for it or not. Marvin Jones touches upon the challenge of forgiving when forgiveness it is not asked for:

> It is a great struggle to forgive those who have wronged us, even though they have not acknowledged the wrong or asked for forgiveness. Joseph's brothers were going about life! They went to Egypt to buy food for their families. Their goal was to return to Canaan and continue to eke out a living.[51]

Before things became troublesome for these boys in Egypt, I am not sure that they were interested in being forgiven at all. They were in Egypt to buy food and get back home, to get back to the mainstream of society and commerce.

Having established the need for forgiving the offender whether they have asked for it or not, I now ask the first question again: "How can I know if I have forgiven my offender?" I suggest that the process of embracing forgiveness has been worked through and is complete when the following aspects are in place:

I. FOR THE REMAINDER OF LIFE, THE OFFENSE AND THE OFFENDER REMAIN A SECRET.

Notice what Joseph does in Genesis 45:1. *"Then Joseph could no longer control himself before all his attendants, and he cried out, 'Have everyone leave my presence!' So there was no one with Joseph when he made himself known to his brothers"* (Genesis 45:1).

Why did Joseph make everybody leave? It is because he is going to persuade his brothers to come and live in Egypt, and he does not want any Egyptian knowing about their past injustice toward him. These brothers are going to be catalysts for the twelve tribes of Israel, and things will be tough for the Hebrews for another four hundred years. They certainly

---

51 Marvin D. Jones, *Joseph, a Man of Integrity: A Homiletical Approach* (Cluj-Napoca, Cluj, Romania: Emanuel University Press, 2008) 115.

do not need to start their lives in Egypt with anyone knowing their past. There is a greater good and a greater need to be considered here than getting even. Joseph protects their secret for the greater good.

Under the leadership of the Holy Spirit, Joseph is orchestrating a process that not only embraces forgiveness, but also leads his brothers to repentance. Why is he willing to do this? Does he see potential in these men who have been poor examples of brothers to this point? Joseph sees a greater good and he has hope that this greater good will emerge. Dick Tibbits talks about how forgiveness and hope are bound up together:

Forgiveness and hope are inseparably linked. In fact, forgiveness gives birth to hope because forgiveness insists that, in the end, it is better to move toward your desired future than to live chained to your unwanted past. That is why you forgive. You don't need to even the score; you simply need to go on with your life. Forgiveness helps you let go of the pain from your past and embrace hope for your future.

Forgiveness also leads to a reorganization of thoughts and a reconstruction of dreams. Forgiveness has the ability to release you from the hurts of your past so you can energetically pursue your future. Forgiveness makes a fresh start in life possible.

Just as your grievance story kept you trapped in the past, it also shapes and defines your future. And that's exactly what your grievance story is doing if you find yourself thinking, "Life is bad now, and it's going to get worse tomorrow."

Forgiveness changes all this. When you revise your grievance story by incorporating a bigger-picture perspective, your past no longer keeps you trapped. But forgiveness doesn't stop at helping you let go of the past. Forgiveness also has the ability to shape your future. Built right into forgiveness is a driving optimism about the future.

Do you see how hope and forgiveness fuel each other? If I have no hope, why should I forgive? And why would I forgive if not for the possibility of gaining something better? That's what hope is all about. Forgiveness and hope march together, arm in arm, in the same parade. When you choose to forgive, you link up with hope and therefore find your way to a brighter future. [52]

Hope for a better future spurs us on to forgive, and the act of forgiving opens up that better future for us; a future where all things become possible. Joseph, no doubt, sees a possibility of a greater future, not only for himself, but also for his brothers and his father. He obviously has hope, but the things hoped for will be deferred if there is no genuine forgiveness. Protection of his brothers and their reputation is a priority to him, and for this reason, he makes all non-family members leave the room.

Often when someone does something wrong to us, the first thing we do is tell someone else. Why is that the case? It is because we cannot tolerate life if the offender is admired, and our object is to minimize their credibility.

Joseph was a hero in Egypt at this time, and he knew that if word leaked out about what his brothers had done to him, all Egypt would hate them. Perhaps he might have relished this idea once, but he is a new person now. He is prime minister because he can be trusted with greatness. Today, God still looks for men and women who can be trusted with greatness to that degree; men and women devoid of bitterness.

It is a good thing when we can bring ourselves to the point of saying, "For the rest of my life, no one will know what this person did to me." There might be two exceptions to the rule of privacy, but they are not because the offender has not been forgiven. One exception would be testifying in a court of law so that justice may be served and protection extended to the public, if it is required. The other exception may be the need to bring it up with a counselor for therapeutic reasons. This should be done with caution, and only with someone who can be trusted. Sometimes people are filled with an idle curiosity, and we may be tempted to share with them what was done to us. We need to avoid people who press us for details for no good reason. If we have truly forgiven, there will be no need to speak about it.

---

52   Dick Tibbits, *Forgive to Live: How Forgiveness Can Save Your Life* (Nashville, TN: Integrity Publishers, 2006) 142-143.

II. FOR THE REMAINDER OF LIFE, THEY WILL NOT BE SUBJECT TO GUILT OR FEAR IN CONNECTION WITH THE OFFENSE.

Convicting is the job of the Holy Spirit, not the one who has been offended. Genesis 45:3–4 is intriguing: *"Joseph said to his brothers, 'I am Joseph! Is my father still living?' But his brothers were not able to answer him, because they were terrified at his presence. Then Joseph said to his brothers, 'Come close to me.' When they had done so, he said, 'I am your brother Joseph, the one you sold into Egypt'"* (Genesis 45:3–4) There is irony here, because once Joseph may have longed to see fear and guilt on their faces; not so now. When they do show fear, his attitude is, "No, you don't understand. Come close to me. I am your brother."

When a person has not really forgiven another, that partial or non-forgiveness will be obvious if the offended person wants the offender to live in fear and trepidation. When a person says, "I want you to know that I forgive you and I accept your apology, but I still remember and I have witnesses, and I am keeping what you wrote in case I may need it someday," then that person has not forgiven even if he thinks he has. The Holy Spirit is not impressed when we try to keep records and a score card.

Furthermore, Joseph did not even want his brothers to feel guilty. He said, *"And now, do not be distressed and do not be angry with yourselves for selling me here, because it was to save lives that God sent me ahead of you"* (Genesis 45:5). Isn't it obvious to you what Joseph is doing? He is setting his brothers free.

To cause another person to live in guilt and remain beholden to you is manipulative and cruel. We would be cold-hearted indeed if we derived enjoyment from nurturing a sense of guilt in the other person. Sadly, some people live a lifetime in that state of mind.

Often the most complex parts of forgiveness are the games people play around the subject. We often like to play "tit-for-tat," and frequently, when a person says, "I forgive you," it is because they have, in fact, not forgiven. They are looking for an opportunity to recount the details, dwell in their pain and stir up guilt feelings in the other. Making the other person feel guilty all over again only proves that forgiveness has not taken place.

III. FOR THE REMAINDER OF LIFE, THE OFFENDER WILL BE ALLOWED TO RETAIN THEIR DIGNITY.

One can almost sense this conversation erupting among the boys:

"Asher, did I hear him right? Did I hear Joseph say that God did this and we didn't?"

"Yes, Levi, that's what he said."

"Naphtali, did I hear him right? Did Joseph say that this was part of God's plan?"

"That's what he said, Issachar."

We can almost hear Joseph interrupting this imaginary conversation with, "Now, don't get me wrong, brothers, you did evil. I am not letting you off the hook from that knowledge. But though you meant it for evil, God used it for good. Yes, you heard me right, Reuben, God made all things work together for good, so take your shame to God, not to me" (paraphrase). That is the best news they could have imagined.

When we have been attacked in word or deed, it is an attack on our essence and on our dignity. As a result, the temptation is to give it back. Shults and Sandage give insight:

> Interpersonal offences present a shaming attack on our dignity as persons, and they activate our ways of facing ourselves. Shame and pride are two interrelated dynamics of the self-system that strongly impact the process of forgiveness. Pride is a positive feeling about the self, and shame is a negative feeling about the self. When someone treats us poorly it can feel like a loss of face and a shameful assault on our pride and self-esteem, and our guard against feelings of vulnerability. Those high in personality traits of shame-proneness and narcissistic pride can be expected to struggle with forgiving others and seeking forgiveness.[53]

---

53   F. LeRon Shults and Steven J. Sandage, *The Face of Forgiveness: Searching for Wholeness and Salvation* (Grand Rapids, MI: Baker Book House Company, 2003) 54-55.

It is rather interesting that, as Shults and Sandage imply, when a person is too proud or shameful to ask for forgiveness, he or she may not readily forgive others. This will be troublesome to the proud or shameful person, and one of the best ways to correct that behavior is to let the offender retain his or her dignity wherever possible.

IV. FORGIVENESS IS A COMMITMENT FOR LIFE.

I am sure you know something about someone that, were you to share it, would destroy that person. Many of us are in that position of knowing. Maybe you intend to tell it, maybe you don't. You never quite make the matter clear with the person. Subtle manipulation is at play.

Isn't it wonderful to know that Jesus does not operate on that premise? How dare any of us, as children of the living God, say we want to have a greater anointing of the Holy Spirit on our life, and yet we subtly threaten someone. It may not be an open and verbal threat, but to hold something over someone in silence is nonetheless a threat. Embracing forgiveness means that the offender is protected from his deepest, darkest secret for life. The devil will always want to point the finger and say, "Look what he did. You've let him off the hook! He's moving on with his life – are you going to let him get away with it? You should stick the knife in and turn it a bit. Just let him feel a little of the hurt you felt."

When you and I refuse to give in to that kind of temptation, we find that there is a healing and a release that is sweet beyond measure. Yes, it is a process, but embracing forgiveness is a life sentence without possibility of parole, and the peace derived is so much better than the pain retained.

These brothers of Joseph just cannot take this in. It is too good to be true. But a certain panic hits them seventeen years after Jacob dies. They make up a story, and it comes out in Genesis 50 when they say to their brother, "Joseph, before our father died he told us to tell you to please forgive us for what we did" (paraphrased).

Joseph begins to cry. He cannot believe what he has heard. He says, "What is the matter with you guys? I told you seventeen years ago that I forgave you. I forgave you then, and I forgive you now. I meant it then, and I mean it now" (paraphrased). Embracing forgiveness is for life. It is intended to be extended at the time of the offense as best as one can and to remain in effect throughout your life and the offender's life.

Some would question whether embracing forgiveness is healthy, reasonable or wise. What about times when the offense is so great that the words "I forgive you" just cannot be uttered? Grace Ketterman and David Hazard offer insight in this regard:

Many today ask, is forgiveness realistic? What good does forgiveness do? And what if the offender has done something so wrong, so hurtful, that it cannot be simply forgiven? Wouldn't society fall into lawless anarchy if criminals were not held responsible for their crimes?

We suspect that people who insist on having answers to such questions are prisoners to a desired outcome in greater measure than they know. They would like to know that their words and actions will control the actions of another and get them what they want sooner or later. These people have missed the point: we do not have the power to control others' actions, and we cannot make them feel remorseful or in need of making soul-restoring recompense for what they have done wrong. This lies beyond our ability.

"Simple forgiveness" is for all those little infractions of life – forgotten anniversaries, thoughtless remarks, and the carelessness that caused spilled milk. In cases where a serious offense has been committed, or a habit of offense has seated itself in someone, forgiveness has to be offered in combination with other responses.

As men and women on the road to maturity, we have to accept that all people are a mixture, and that many situations will require us to mix forgiveness with some other response as well. Simple forgiveness will not do. The best change for "good" to occur will come from learning to balance several impulses at once.

This is not quite as complicated as it sounds. In fact, every one of us experiences complicated feelings. What we need is a way to sort them out and prioritize them. [54]

Embracing forgiveness is an inner state and invisible to the world; only its effects are visible. How are we to understand this inner state of forgiveness? Probably the best way to view it is in light of the One who is capable of completely forgiving. Gary Chapman helps with defining God's forgiveness:

Three Hebrew words and four Greek words are translated *forgive* in the English Scriptures. They are basically synonyms with slightly varying shades of meaning. The key ideas are to cover, to take away, to pardon, and to be gracious to. The most common of these is the idea of taking away one's sins. For example, the psalmist says, "As far as the east is from the west, so far has He removed our transgressions from us" (Psalm 103:12). Thus, God's forgiveness is relieving the person from God's judgment – from the penalty due the sinner. Again the psalmist says, "He does not treat us as our sins deserve or repay us according to our iniquities" Psalm 103:10). Isaiah the prophet spoke of God "blotting out" our sins and remembering them no more against us" (Isaiah 43:25). Clearly God's forgiveness means that our sins no longer stand as a barrier between us and God. Forgiveness removes the distance and allows us open fellowship with God.[55]

Our embracing of forgiveness should model the forgiveness of God that is described above.

Finally, is there a danger with embracing forgiveness? Does embracing forgiveness mean that the offended party no longer draws a boundary separating themselves from a sinful lifestyle or toxic individuals? As Spiros Zodhiates explains, toxicity must be removed from our lives:

---

54 Grace Ketterman and David Hazard, *When You Can't Say "I Forgive You"* (Colorado Springs, CO: NavPress, 2000) 54-55.

55 Gary Chapman, *The Other Side of Love: Handling Anger in a Godly Way* (Chicago, IL: Moody Press, 1999) 105.

For a Believer to fall into sin is bad enough, but to tolerate it as something acceptable by God and the congregation of local Believers is far worse. This was the weakness of the Corinthian church, and unfortunately it is the situation of the church of the twentieth century [written in 1992]. How many local congregations today have the moral courage and spiritual insight to put out of their midst a flagrant sinner?[56]

Furthermore, as it relates to the individual's need to forgive, Dwight Carlson talks about how to process offenses:

Often people have misconceptions about what forgiveness really is. Many of us, when trying to forgive someone, try to talk ourselves into thinking that what the other person did wasn't really wrong, or that he didn't really mean to do it, or that we overreacted to what he did. This may sometimes be the case, but at other times we need to fully recognize that what the other person did was definitely wrong, but that we will nevertheless forgive him or her and forget it, no matter how much he or she has hurt us.

Forgiving means that we actively choose to give up our grudge despite the severity of the injustice done to us. It does not mean that we have to say or feel, "That didn't hurt me," or "It didn't really matter." Some things may hurt very much, and we must not deny that fact, but after fully recognizing the hurt, we should choose to forgive.[57]

You might conclude from all of this that such forgiveness comes at too great a cost. For an unsaved person, it may indeed feel so. However, for the child of God, such bitterness is inexcusable, as Spurgeon points out:

O you who know the Lord, put up earnest and silent prayers just now, that my message may come home with power to troubled consciences; and I beseech you, for your own profit, look back to the

---

56 Spiros Zodhiates, *Immorality: Can We Sweep It Under the Rug?* (Chattanooga, TN: AMG Publishers, 1992) 92-93.

57 Dwight L. Carlson, *Overcoming Hurts & Anger* (Eugene, OR: Harvest House Publishers, 1981) 125-126.

hole of the pit whence ye were digged, and to the miry clay whence ye were drawn, and remember how God received you. And while we talk of what he is willing and able to do to the far off sinners, let your souls leap with joyous gratitude at the recollection of how he received you into his love, and made you partakers of his grace in days gone by. [58]

If we conclude that embracing forgiveness is too costly, then maybe we should count the cost of not embracing forgiveness. In the words of our Lord Himself, *"For if you forgive other people when they sin against you, your heavenly Father will also forgive you. But if you do not forgive others their sins, your Father will not forgive your sins"* (Matthew 6:14–15).

---

58   Charles H. Spurgeon, *Twelve Sermons on the Prodigal Son Delivered at the Metropolitan Tabernacle* (Grand Rapids, MI: Baker Book House, 1980 reprint) 87.

CHAPTER SEVEN

JOSEPH'S DEFINING MOMENT:
EMBRACING HIS DELIGHTED FATHER

Often Christians make the mistake of thinking that God cannot bless, improve, or work through dysfunction. The belief is, "When I get my act together and get my life cleaned up, then maybe God can do something." While it may be true that God will bless when we confess sin and ask His forgiveness, we should never make the mistake of thinking that God cannot bless in the midst of dysfunction. God is capable of anything, and the entire Bible is a redemptive story of God blessing in spite of and because of mankind's dysfunction.

If anyone needs proof of that, one only needs to cast an eye on the family of Jacob, his two wives and concubines, his twelve sons and his daughter. Left alone, Jacob was a walking time bomb. He lived in fear. He was terrified that either his father-in-law Laban would find and kill him, or that if Laban did not kill him, Esau would.

Jacob had a hole in his heart. Consequently, so did his beloved son, Joseph. Many Christians live this way. Max Lucado graphically illustrates the scenario where we are all a part of a traumatic nightmare, just like the one in the *Exxon Valdez* tragedy. Lucado creates an apt metaphor of the collision that the oil freighter had on March 29, 1989 and the oil spill that occurred in Prince William Sound of Alaska. Lucado uses this collision and tragedy as an illustration of the traumas we perpetrate upon one another in his book *The Applause of Heaven,* in a chapter entitled "The Father in the Face of the Enemy."

"The collision, terrible as it was, was mild compared to the ones that occur daily in our relationships. You've been there. Someone doesn't meet your expectations. Promises go unfulfilled. Verbal pistols are drawn, and a round of words is fired.

"The result? A collision of the hull of your heart against the reef of someone's actions. Precious energy escapes, coating the surface of your soul with the deadly film of resentment. A black blanket of bitterness darkens your world, dims your sight, sours your outlook, and suffocates your joy.

"Do you have a hole in your heart?" [59]

Jacob's entire life was like that. He has been hit with one blow after another. Interestingly, Joseph's life was like that too, as has been discovered. The difference is that Joseph seems to have had insight into his own pain and the pain in others. Rare and special is the person who has this insight. Thank God for people who can focus on something other than the dark side of their own existence and see the tragic times that others are going through, who can get beyond their own pain and have compassion on another hurting heart. Sad it is that too many people just do not have the skill set and emotional makeup to get to the place where Joseph was.

Such is the heart of a hurting wife after quarreling with her husband, as Marjorie Holmes Mighell reveals in her prayer to God:

God, we quarreled again last night, and today my heart is sore. My heart is heavy. It is literally heavy, as if a leaden weight were hanging in my breast.

And part of its weight is that he is bowed with it too. I keep seeing him, his head low, his shoulders actually bowed under it as he trudged off to work.

I can hardly bear the image. I could hardly bear it then. I wanted to run out and stop him, saying nothing is worth this awful estrangement, and say I'm sorry. But I didn't. I let him go, afraid more words might only lead to more quarreling.

I turned my sore heart back into this house, so heavily haunted by the quarrel. I drag myself about my tasks here, trying to forget the things we said.

---

59   Max Lucado, *The Applause of Heaven* (Dallas, TX: Word, 1990) 108.

But the words keep battering away at my sore heart and aching head. However I try to turn them off, they repeat themselves incessantly, a kind of idiot re-enactment of a play so awful that you keep trying to run out of the theater. Only all the exits are locked. The play goes on and on – and the worst of it is I keep adding more lines to it, trying to improve my part in it, adding things I wish I'd said.

God of love, please let this play end! Open the exits of my mind. Let the blessed daylight of forgiveness and forgetting pour in.

Bless him wherever he is. Lift the weight of this quarrel from his heart, his shoulders. I claim peace for him now, this minute. I claim and confirm your peace and joy for both of us when he returns. [60]

That is a heart that is hurting, yet able to see the wounds in another's heart as well. That is a heart that is refusing to let go of the soul she loves. She may have disagreed with him about something, but her heart is large enough to make room for and embrace forgiveness. Such was the kind of man that Joseph was. And because Joseph gave his life to that kind of forgiving spirit, his brothers, while still pagans, experienced the blessings of God.

God will bless dysfunctional families even in the midst of dysfunction. Many have been the times that a believer in Jesus, living in a family of unbelievers, is blessed of God, and others in the household have benefitted from those blessings, which run off the believer and splash abundantly about onto all who are close.

God will also bless a family who loves one another, and Joseph loved his brothers and his father. As the story concludes, we see that Joseph keeps his promise not to seek revenge on them, and he keeps that promise for the remainder of his life. God will also bless a family in order to be a blessing to other families.

---

60   Marjorie Holmes Mighell, *Lord Let Me Love: A Marjorie Holmes Treasury* (Garden City, NY: Doubleday & Company, Inc., 1978) 26.

Jacob is seen as having arrived in Egypt, and in Genesis 47:10 it says, *"Then Jacob blessed Pharaoh and went out from his presence"* (Genesis 47:10a). Here is an old man at the age of one hundred and thirty years, not receiving a blessing from the king, but blessing the most powerful potentate in the world, and none of that would have happened had Joseph not exercised genuine forgiveness. Jacob would have died an unhappy man, believing that Joseph was dead, and those undeserving ten brothers (plus one innocent brother in Benjamin) would have starved to death.

The boys come back from Egypt and tell their father that Joseph is alive and is the prime minister, and Jacob does not believe them. Genesis 45:26 says, *"But he [Jacob] was stunned, for he did not believe them"* (Genesis 45:26b NASB). John MacArthur says, "When Jacob heard the news that his son Joseph was still alive, he was so stunned that his heart momentarily stopped."[61] It is believed that at that moment, Jacob may have had a heart attack or slight stroke. But when Jacob saw the wagons that were sent for him and all the entourage of Egypt that had come to retrieve the family, he believed their story and regained his strength. Later on, during the journey to Egypt, the Lord confirms to Jacob that going on this trip to Egypt is the right action to take.

Jacob arrives in Goshen, and Joseph gets in his chariot and goes to meet his father. When his father sees him, Jacob says, *"Now I am ready to die, since I have seen for myself that you are still alive"* (Genesis 46:30). That is a delighted father.

Because of Joseph's obedience and forgiveness, and because of the sovereignty of God, Jacob, who had a hard life and a sinful past, ends up a delighted and embracing father, and Joseph receives more defining moments in his life as a result of being reunited with his father.

Joseph may seemingly have dealt harshly with his brothers when they approached him asking for grain, but reconciliation, not banishment, was his ultimate goal in the process of forgiveness. The kind of forgiveness that Joseph embraced and extended in order to see a delighted father meant that there had to be reconciliation at all costs. Yes, there is always a cost to reconciliation, as David Augsburger points out.

---

61 John MacArthur, *Twelve Unlikely Heroes* (Nashville, TN: Thomas Nelson, Inc., 2012) 37.

If genuine reconciliation seems a rare event, it is because authentic love is uncommon as well. Love, when it is true agape, is an equal regard that includes love of enemy. In the situation of alienation, the other is an opponent, at enmity and therefore the enemy. Agape refuses that definition and sees the other as estranged but not excluded. The nature of agape is inclusion.

If the goal of genuine reconciliation is joining with the other, then the movement toward concord may begin with sharpening discord. Peacemaking may be at first conflict-making. This does not feel "Christian" since it does not allow for the degree of denial, accommodation, and "niceness" necessary to "Christian" behavior. Confrontation with clear differentiation precedes union with authentic connection.

The truth will set you free, but first it sets you right side up, and that is often the reverse of the position when one is defending a dispute. One must return from self-defensive withdrawal and re-approach the opponent; one must reverse both the self-justifications and the accusations against the offender by risking openness and practicing empathy. The necessary union of empathy and exploration – for disputants and those who mediate – offers the two faces of respect. Respect has two aspects, empathy for the other's feelings, perspectives, and capacities, and a challenge to fully responsible behavior. [62]

Having paid that price to reconcile, Joseph will now see his father as a man who has been healed from his past. How is it that Jacob ends his life as a delighted and embracing father? There are various areas of Jacob's life that result in his peaceful and contented final years, and Joseph benefits from all of them:

JACOB LEAVES A TESTIMONY.
As was earlier discussed, Jacob has had a difficult life. Yet he is able to leave a testimony concerning his walk with the Lord that will act as a legacy for

---

62   David W. Augsburger, *Helping People Forgive* (Louisville, KY: Westminster John Knox Press, 1996) 158.

his sons and grandsons. He is able to point to two specific experiences that were turning points for him, experiences that are a testimony to his very real relationship with the Lord. He recounts these to Joseph as they reconnect after those lost years.

First, Jacob gives a testimony concerning a salvation experience. *"Then Jacob said to Joseph, 'God Almighty appeared to me at Luz in the land of Canaan and blessed me, and He said to me, 'Behold, I will make you fruitful and numerous, and I will make you a company of peoples, and will give this land to your descendants after you for an everlasting possession'"* (Genesis 48:34 NASB). God has made Jacob one of His very own, and as an old man approaching death at the age of one hundred forty-seven, Jacob tells Joseph that in spite of all the hardships, "Son, I want you to know that I am a follower of God and I can point back to a specific time and place where this became fact" (paraphrased).

Jacob also gives a testimony concerning a spiritual experience. *"And he blessed Joseph, and said, God, before whom my fathers Abraham and Isaac did walk, the God which fed me all my life long unto this day, the Angel which redeemed me from all evil ..."* (Genesis 48:15–16a *KJV*). Remember the time when Jacob wrestled with the angel, and notice that the word *Angel* is capitalized? That Angel he wrestled with was none other than the Son of God, the second Person in the Trinity, Jesus. Jacob walked away from that experience a marked man.

Can a man ever encounter Jesus Christ and walk away unchanged? Many would say yes, he can. But therein lies the definition of the word *changed.* Many encounter Jesus and reject him, but they are still changed, albeit in a negative way. Jacob had a fresh, new and unique experience, not to be confused with a second blessing as many believe that wrestling was, but as in an experience like he had never known before or known was possible. When Jacob wrestled with God and left a marked man at Bethel, Jacob knew that he had encountered none other than Almighty God.

In addition to his testimony concerning two unique experiences with the Lord, Jacob gives a testimony concerning his love for his wife, Rachel.

Is there any sweeter love story in the Bible than the story of Jacob and his love for Rachel? Rachel has been gone a long time, but as he talks with Joseph after all these years, he remembers the love of his life. *"Now as for me, when I came from Paddan, Rachel died, to my sorrow, in the land of Canaan on the journey, when there was still some distance to go to Ephrath; and I buried her there on the way to Ephrath (that is, Bethlehem)"* (Genesis 48:7 NASB). Notice the phrase *to my sorrow.* In the sparse language of the Old Testament, this recalling of a deep love does not embellish or elaborate; as always, short phrases reveal much. He is saying, "Oh Joseph, how I loved your mother and how I miss her" (paraphrased).

Listen to love speaking in a quite different context: Here is General Douglas MacArthur giving his final farewell speech at West Point after a long and illustrious career. It is one of the greatest speeches in history. Towards the end of his speech, he speaks about his love for the Corps of West Point:

> The shadows are lengthening for me. The twilight is here. My days of old have vanished - tone and tints. They have gone glimmering through the dreams of things that were. Their memory is one of wondrous beauty, watered by tears and coaxed and caressed by the smiles of yesterday. I listen then, but with thirsty ear, for the witching melody of faint bugles blowing Reveille, of far drums beating the long roll.
>
> In my dreams I hear again the crash of guns, the rattle of musketry, the strange, mournful mutter of the battlefield. But in the evening of my memory, I come back to West Point. Always there echoes and re-echoes: Duty, Honor, Country.
>
> Today marks my final roll call with you. But I want you to know that when I cross the river, my last conscious thoughts will be of the Corps, and the Corps, and the Corps. [63]

63   Douglas MacArthur, "General Douglas MacArthur's Farewell Speech: Given to the Corps of Cadets at West Point, May 12, 1962," MacArthur Farewell: The National Center for Public Policy Research, entry posted, n.d., http://www.nationalcenter.org/MacArthurFarewell.html [accessed October 30, 2012].

What an incredible speech. The word pictures painted here of a life nearing its end and a love recalled are apt for Jacob too. Could he be saying, "Son, I loved your mother so much that in the evening of my memory, my last conscious thoughts will be of Rachel, and of Rachel, and of Rachel"? (paraphrased). He is giving a testimony of the marital love he had for Joseph's mother.

These three things – Jacob's lifelong walk with Lord, his unique personal encounter with the Lord and his love for Joseph's mother – have left a testimony on Jacob's lips, and he recounts them now for his son and grandsons. Forever those grandchildren would know that Granddad, despite his personal troubles, definitely had known the Lord, and for the remainder of his life, he would no longer agree to living an apathetic life with God.

In addition to his personal experiences with God and his love for his wife, Jacob leaves a testimony concerning God's providential care throughout his life. A careful examination of Jacob's early life will reveal that, when young, Jacob was selfish and self-centered. He does not see life from the same perspective anymore. Jacob says, *"... the God which fed me all my life long unto this day ..."* (Genesis 48:15b *KJV*). God had been providing for Jacob even when Jacob was not aware of it.

Have you ever gone through an experience and looked back later noticing that God has been providing for you even when you were not aware of it? Perhaps if we as Christians recognized that God is providing for us, Jesus is interceding for us and the Holy Spirit is present in every situation, working to unite us to the Father, we would recognize the awesome hand of God in our circumstances. If we could see the spiritual and physical manna that God provides for us, and most of all, see the forgiveness that God has extended to us – if we could keep it all in view – how much easier we would find it to forgive others; we might more easily welcome our circumstances and embrace forgiveness.

When we fail to recognize the providential hand of God on our life, we will more easily accept the world's philosophy regarding forgiveness, such as this fallacy being taught today:

Forgiveness is not always possible, nor is reconciliation. They are concepts grounded largely in religion that, depending on the situation, may require a level of compassion or a brand of spirituality that many of us do not have; or they may require an effort many of us are not prepared to make. As a friend and daughter of Holocaust survivors suggested, sometimes it may make sense to hold on to outrage. Some would argue that certain wrongs can only be repaid with revenge.[64]

The problem with that line of thinking is that it is entirely worldly, entirely devoid of Christ. God told us believers not to judge and not to seek revenge. We do not have sufficient facts to judge and we simply do not know how to deal justly with offense. God says for us to leave it to Him. When a person exacts judgment and seeks to repay, he will either dish out too much or too little repayment. It is God's job to deal with those who hurt and destroy, not ours, and the believer cannot, therefore, concur with the above statement of Cose. If the child of God could just see how God is moving and providing for his life, he would know that God will continue to provide and will right all wrongs in due time.

Jacob so beautifully recognizes that God has fed him all of his life up until the day he speaks these words. That simple recognition is a testimony.

Last, Jacob leaves a testimony concerning the sovereignty of God in all of his affairs.

Throughout this incredible story of Joseph's life, we have seen how wise and insightful Joseph has been. In every scene we read, he is the one who stands out for godliness and wisdom. Yet for all his wisdom, Joseph is still not totally aware of all that God is doing. In the last encounter we read of between Joseph and his father, Jacob passes on a strange blessing to his son and grandsons, one which even Joseph does not fully understand. God is still working in Joseph's life through his own father, Jacob, in order to make of Joseph's life a redemptive story of love and grace.

---

64 Ellis Cose, *Bone to Pick: Of Forgiveness, Reconciliation, Reparation, and Revenge* (New York, NY: Atria Books, 2004) 19.

Reuben will not be the father of a Hebrew tribe; the people who come from his line will be absorbed into the tribe of Judah. Levi will inherit no land, and although his descendants will be called Levites, they will not be a tribe. They will remain, however, a very integral part of the Hebrew nation. Even Joseph will not have a tribe named after him.

To make up for these losses, Joseph has two sons, Manasseh, the oldest, and Ephraim, the youngest. Prior to Jacob's passing, he does two things for these boys that are noteworthy. Through these actions, we begin to see how central this story has been for the furtherance of the Hebrew nation. Manasseh and Ephraim will become two of the tribes of Israel. What if Joseph had never gone to Egypt and never married? What if Joseph had never forgiven his brothers, never been reunited with them, and as a result Jacob had never pronounced a blessing upon these two grandchildren of his and adopted them? We could speculate a great deal; one thing we may be certain of is that these last events, which could never have taken place without Joseph's decisions, are crucial to the nation of Israel.

Jacob adopts his grandsons as if they are his own sons. He tells Joseph, *"Now your two sons, who were born to you in the land of Egypt before I came to you in Egypt, are mine; Ephraim and Manasseh shall be mine, as Reuben and Simeon are"* (Genesis 48:5a NASB). It was not that Joseph was not properly caring for these boys. Joseph had, at his disposal, the very finest that Egypt could offer. In modern times and current culture, it is thought that when a person adopts a child, it is because the biological parents are not able or willing to care for the child. This is not the case with Joseph. Jacob recognizes something that God is doing, and even Joseph does not yet understand it.

God has orchestrated so much more than the prevention of starvation in this family. He has been organizing His nation of people. God promised He would do this, and now is making good on that promise. This was the nation that God had promised Jacob's grandfather, Abraham. These two boys, Manasseh and Ephraim, will make up the two tribes that would be missed, thus giving us the twelve complete tribes. Jacob continues by saying, *"Any children born to you after them will be yours; in the territory they inherit they will be reckoned under the names of their brothers"* (Genesis 48:6). He is saying that any future offspring born to Joseph will belong to Joseph, but these two boys will be his, Jacob's. He is not taking them away from Joseph as much as he is claiming them spiritually. Jacob is placing the boys in line with his own sons, so that whatever blessings come to his sons will too fall upon Manasseh and Ephraim.

Jacob is about to bless his grandsons, but he first enquires about the boys. *"When Israel saw Joseph's sons, he said, 'Who are these?' Joseph said to his father, 'They are my sons, whom God has given me here.' So he said, 'Bring them to me, please, that I may bless them.' Now the eyes of Israel were so dim from age that he could not see. Then Joseph brought them close to him, and he kissed them and embraced them"* (Genesis 48:8-10 NASB).

Do you notice that a strange, unusual and yet very familiar incident takes place as the story continues? It is reminiscent of a time when Jacob was blessed instead of his own brother, Esau. Jacob is almost blind, or may be totally blind. He places his hand on the boys to pronounce a blessing on them. Instead of blessing the eldest first, his right hand moves across to where Ephraim, the youngest is standing, and Jacob pronounces his blessing on him. Joseph thinks this is a mistake and tries to guide his father's hand back to Manasseh, telling his father that he has his hand on the wrong boy. Jacob rebukes Joseph's correction. Joseph had good intentions, but as was pointed out earlier, even with all of his wisdom, he is not aware that God is the one who is doing the choosing.

Moses, in his writing of Genesis, recounts the story, *"Joseph said to him, 'No, my father, this one is the firstborn; put your right hand on his head.' But his father refused and said, 'I know, my son, I know. He too will become a people, and he too will become great. Nevertheless, his younger brother will be greater than he, and his descendants will become a group of nations"* (Genesis 48:18–19). Consequently, in subsequent verses, the reader will notice that the names are now switched. Ephraim will be listed before Manasseh even though Manasseh was the oldest.

Doesn't Jacob know better? In that culture, it was the oldest who received the greater blessing. Why is Jacob going against culture? It is because God cares very little for culture, and Jacob is bearing testimony to the fact that God does the choosing.

In almost all cultures, the oldest is revered as the inheritor of the greater blessing. Even today, people talk about "my first born," or "my first-born son." It has less meaning in a more modern Western culture than it did in more primitive Eastern and Middle Eastern cultures of Biblical times, but it is still common to revere the oldest as the one whom God has greatly blessed. Yet in this instance, God is showing us that in His economy, there is a different standard.

There are other instances in Scripture where this is also seen. Jacob himself was a deceiver who stole his older brother's birthright and received his older brother's blessing by subterfuge, yet God blessed him in spite of his wrong doing. Joseph also was not the first born; the first born of his siblings, Reuben, never quite stepped into his role as eldest and leader, though God still blessed him in spite of his failings. David, the king of Israel, was the youngest boy of Jesse. Solomon, the wisest man who ever lived, was also not the first born in David's line.

Jacob may have no physical sight at this time, but it is obvious that in place of sight, God has given him insight. Even the wise Joseph has no insight on this particular occasion.

God is no respecter of persons, and all of us stand on level ground when we come to the foot of the cross of Jesus Christ. This story should be a testimony to every believer today. God can bless a person who is the oldest; God can bless a middle child; and God can also bless the youngest. God is sovereign.

Why does God bless the oldest in many families, the middle child in some families and the youngest in other families? It has little to do with position in the family and much to do with the commitment of that person's heart. Here in Jacob's offspring, we see twelve boys and one girl, and only one of them walked with God until the very end. In the final instance, however, we cannot speak categorically of why this or that happens; the only answer that really makes sense is that God is sovereign and the choosing is up to Him. This brings to mind the passage where the Apostle Paul said, *"For consider your calling, brethren, that there were not many wise according to the flesh, not many mighty, not many noble; but God has chosen the foolish things of the world to shame the wise, and God has chosen the weak things of the world to shame the things which are strong, and the base things of the world and the despised God has chosen, the things that are not, so that He may nullify the things that are, so that "no man may boast before God"* (1 Corinthians 1:26–29). God does the choosing, and He does it for our good, and ultimately for His glory.

ETERNAL CONSEQUENCES

The most remarkable thing about this story is that none of this would have taken place had it not been for the full forgiveness that was birthed in one man, Joseph. Had Joseph never forgiven his brothers, he would never have sent them to bring Jacob back with them to Egypt. He would never have seen his father again and never seen Benjamin. His sons would never have known anything of the true nature of forgiveness and moreover, they would never have been blessed and adopted by their grandfather Jacob.

When we just cannot or will not forgive, there are eternal consequences, most of which we will never know. Because Joseph forgave, situations and circumstances were orchestrated that could never have been imagined and that reverberate to our current day. Had those two boys never have been blessed and adopted by Jacob, the twelve tribes of Israel, one of which produced the earthly lineage of Jesus, might never have come into being and the Hebrew nation could possibly have become extinct. Obviously, this is not certain because we have already established that God is sovereign and that God can do as He pleases using methods of His own choosing, but there is no doubt that God has orchestrated all of these events.

Joseph's family never became a tribe, but because of his forgiveness, twelve tribes were born, two of which took their names from Joseph's boys. Suffice it to say, Joseph received abundant defining moments after his reunion with his father due to his embraced and extended forgiveness; not the least of which was simply seeing and being embraced again by his delighted father. Isn't it true that God cares for the littlest, the least and the last?

CONCLUSION

WHEN FORGIVENESS IS EMBRACED, GRACE ABOUNDS

Forgiveness embraced bears many faces. This invisible and humanly impossible dynamic of forgiveness has always triggered this question in my mind and heart: What does forgiveness really look like? The process by which we arrive at a place of forgiveness may be as varied as the individuals who embrace it and, in addition, the degree of forgiveness extended may also vary. Yet there is a common denominator to all – all humans have had, or will experience, the need to be forgiven. Furthermore, outside of those who die while still in infancy, no human leaves this life without having needed to forgive someone at some point. Forgiveness, traveling both ways, is common to every soul on earth.

Although forgiveness is a fundamental tenet of the Christian faith, its truths are taught in some fashion in most every religion; hence the claim that *all* humans must deal with forgiveness without exception. Many religions incorporate forgiveness in their doctrine. For example, Mormonism includes this teaching in its statutes, as the late Spencer Kimball, the former prophet and president of The Church of Jesus Christ of Latter-day Saints, discussed in his book *The Miracle of Forgiveness.* Kimball wrote, "... man naturally ponders: how can I best secure that forgiveness? One of the many basic factors stands out as indispensable immediately: one must forgive to be forgiven."[65]

Forgiveness leaves no one, no religion, and no people-group untouched. Consequently, there are two kinds of people in this world; those who embrace and extend forgiveness and those who do not.

Yet many would question whether forgiveness is even possible, because nothing on earth moves backwards. You cannot undo something.

---

65   Spencer W. Kimball, *The Miracle of Forgiveness* (Salt Lake City, UT: Bookcraft, Inc., 1969) 261.

You cannot unsay something. You cannot un-hear something. Humanity, from the beginning of time, has been set up by natural and moral laws and codes, and those laws and codes are firmly and divinely established and cannot be changed. However, H.D. McDonald would disagree:

> For even the ordering of the natural realm by law does not prohibit God's further and special acting. True, nature does behave in regular fashion according to certain laws. But then, as Karl Barth declares, "We cannot hypostatize the concept of law." Laws are not the final factor in the universe. Behind the interlocking system of nature is a personal God who can act directly in His own universe and can inaugurate irregular happenings in the broad scheme of regular events.[66]

McDonald is accurate. Forgiveness from God and forgiveness between people is one of those irregular happenings. Embracing and extending forgiveness and completely forgiving one another is possible when God is brought into the equation. For us, apart from the work of God, forgiveness remains nebulous and insufficient. But with God, full forgiveness is possible.

So how does this forgiveness happen? We have established that embracing forgiveness is a process. As we draw towards the conclusion of our time together through this book, my question remains; how can we genuinely extend forgiveness so that grace may abound?

There are some erroneous aspects to the process of forgiveness that delay its achievement. Lewis Smedes labels a chapter "Some Nice Things Forgiving Is Not" in his book entitled *Forgive and Forget: Healing the Hurts We Don't Deserve.* He says that forgiving is not forgetting, which is an interesting thought, because the title of the book gives the impression that forgiving and forgetting go hand in hand. Nevertheless, he submits this point:

---

66   Karl Barth, *Church Dogmatics* (Edinburgh, UK: T&T Clark, 1975), 3.3:129, quoted in
      H.D. McDonald, *Forgiveness and Atonement* (Grand Rapids, MI: Baker Book House,
      1984) 18.

When we forgive someone, we do not forget the hurtful act, as if forgetting came along with the forgiveness package, the way strings come with a violin. Begin with basics. If you forget, you will not forgive at all. You can never forgive people for things you have forgotten about. You need to forgive precisely because you have not forgotten what someone did; your memory keeps the pain alive long after the actual hurt has stopped. Remembering is your storage of pain. It is why you need to be healed in the first place.

Forgetting, in fact, may be a dangerous way to escape the inner surgery of the heart that we call forgiving. There are two kinds of pain that we forget. We forget the hurts too trivial to bother about. We forget pains too horrible for our memory to manage.[67]

The above is probably the most memorable quote in the book. I love what Smedes says: "If you forget, you will not forgive at all. You can never forgive people for things you have forgotten about. You need to forgive precisely because you have not forgotten what someone did." The very fact that we remember allows us to walk through the process of forgiveness. Part of that process is not forgetting, but in fact remembering. I would encourage you to read that quote again before you attempt forgiveness of something very hurtful. Smedes' advice is powerful.

Having said that, there is a fine line that we must walk with this issue of forgetting and forgiveness. Although we are not required to forget, neither are we deliberately forced to hold onto memories of pain and injustice. A deliberate coddling of these memories will easily slip us back into resentment. We remember because we are human beings. Yet once we forgive, our memories are overladen with a divine touch and are forever after linked with the balm of forgiveness. It may be natural for us to remember, but when someone makes the statement, "I will forgive, but I won't forget," it is often evidence that genuine forgiveness has not and rarely intends to take place. So the first thing we need to remember is that forgiving does not necessarily mean a lapse in memory.

---

67   Lewis B. Smedes, *Forgive and Forget: Healing the Hurts We Don't Deserve* (San Francisco, CA: Harper & Row Publishers, 1984) 38-39.

In further consideration of what forgiveness is not, Presson and Colter's input must be examined in which they indicate some hindrances to forgiveness. They list five imposters of forgiveness that make one think one has forgiven, when in fact forgiveness may still be a long way off:

There are several "faces" we commonly put on forgiveness. We call these imposters because they misrepresent true forgiveness. True forgiveness is not associated with these imposters. Forgiveness is often misunderstood and, consequently, rejected as an option because of these forgiveness imposters.

Imposter #1: Forgiveness Forgets – When we closely link forgiveness with some form of amnesia, we discredit forgiveness as an option because we know that we can never truly forget.

Imposter #2: Forgiveness Denies – Authentic forgiveness does not deny the hurt and ignore the anger.

Imposter #3: Forgiveness Minimizes – Forgiveness does not minimize the offense. It doesn't say, "Don't worry about it; it's no big deal."

Imposter #4: Forgiveness Excuses – Forgiveness does not bypass the arduous journey by saying, "Oh, I know you didn't mean any harm." Toughen up, and don't just excuse the offender. Yes, the person may have meant to harm you in some way. And that is not all right.

Imposter #5: Forgiveness Restores – Forgiveness does not always restore a relationship to what it once was. Sometimes a restoration is either not possible or not wise.[68]

R.T. Kendall further expounds on the issue of Imposter #3, minimizing the offense, in the context of Jesus' teaching, and he includes this thought in his book *The Sermon on the Mount:*

Some people think they have totally forgiven people because they deny to themselves what really happened. Those who have been raped, been abused in childhood, witnessed a murder or been in a

---

68   Ramon Presson and Ben Colter, *Radical Reconciliation: The Journey of Forgiveness* (Nashville, TN: Serendipity House, 2006) 27.

tragic accident will sometimes live in denial. They sincerely believe they have forgiven, when in fact they deny to themselves what happened. They say, "What they did to me could not have been that bad" – and they live as though nothing happened. That is not total forgiveness.

It is truly forgiveness when you fully realize, accept and calculate what people did – *and then you forgive them.* That is what we are required to do. Not to live in denial but fully know what they did – and still let them off the hook. That is what Jesus means by love.[69]

So forgetting, living in denial, minimizing, excusing and wrongfully restoring a relationship do not necessarily prove that forgiveness has taken place. In each one of these, the object is not the Lord Jesus Christ and the Holy Spirit has not overseen the process. These imposters do not incorporate God's supernatural power. Nancy Leigh DeMoss gives copious detail on a process and plan that has helped her and may be worth examining:

I want to suggest three practical steps you can take – both to accelerate and cement your forgiveness of others. I don't mean to suggest that forgiveness is easy or to reduce it to a three step formula. I realize that painful memories, emotions, and relationships may all be involved and may require further healing.

But I have found these steps helpful for jump-starting that process and setting people on the journey to freedom.

As a starting place in the pathway of forgiveness, *(1) identify the people who have wronged you and the way(s) they have sinned against you.*

Here's a simple way to do that: take a blank sheet of paper and draw two lines from top to bottom, forming three even columns down the page. In the left column, write the names of all those who have sinned against you, anyone with whom you still have unresolved issues of the heart.

---

69   R.T. Kendall, *The Sermon on the Mount* (Minneapolis, MN: Chosen-Baker Publishing Group, 2011) 162.

You know who they are. Mother, father, stepparent, brother, sister, former employer, former pastor, neighbor, son or daughter, ex-mate – make the list.

Then in the middle column – next to the names you've just listed – write out the specific offense (or offenses) each one has committed against you. How did they wrong you? Be specific.

"Wait," you may wonder, "what's the point of bringing all this stuff back up again? I thought we were supposed to 'forgive and forget.' To bury these things. Now you're telling me to list it all!"

It's important to realize that forgiveness does not mean pretending that the offense never happened. That's not honest. That's denial. True forgiveness is not about mind games and dream worlds – it's not about escaping from reality. It's about *facing* reality and dealing with it God's way.

These things that others did to you were wrong. They have hurt you. And God does not want you to run away from your pain but to run to Him in the midst of your pain – to fly head-on into the full fury of it, to face it, to let Him meet you right where it hurts and give you the grace to be set free from any bondage to that hurt.

But one important disclaimer here: in encouraging you to list the ways others have sinned against you, I am not suggesting that you should try dredging up things from your past that you have no memory of, as some would counsel. God is able – and sometimes chooses – to erase painful memories from our minds. There is no value – in fact, I think much harm can be done – in conjuring up memories that God may have mercifully removed.

If there's someone you need to forgive, you probably won't need to go hunting to know who it is and why. Deal with the issues you know need to be dealt with, and the ones that are clear in your mind, and trust the Lord to bring to mind any other offenses you may need to forgive.

Write down any inflicted wounds from the past or present that you are consciously aware of. Don't hide from these. See them for the genuine sins they are.

Now, some would perhaps stop right here. They would think that the mere process of naming those who have wounded you would be healing enough. They might even suggest that you burn this list in the fireplace, symbolically letting all the pain and suffering go up in smoke.

But I believe the Bible leads us to do something else, something deeper, something more healing and holy – *(2) Make sure your conscience is clear toward each of the individuals on your list.*

That's what the third column on your paper is for. Ask yourself, "How have I responded to this person?" Then record your answer. Have you blessed them? Have you loved them? Have you prayed for them? Have you forgiven them?

Or would it be more honest to say that you have withheld love from them, resented them, and been angry with them?[70]

DeMoss continues that often the offended actually becomes an offender in response to the original offense if great care is not taken.

As we have seen in Joseph's life, he followed a life-long pattern in regard to his relationship with his brothers that could be summed up in the words, *choose, chose* and *choice.* The choices he made breathed a formula for a life of grace. One could sum up the formula by calculating: *A choice to embrace forgiveness + forgiveness extended = grace to one another and mercy from God.*

Before looking at how Joseph fleshed this out, the question of "why" must be answered. Why is it so necessary to put in the effort, energy and time to forgive? Quite often, would it not be more productive to just move on and forget that person because of the awful things they have done, labeling them as toxic to one's life? Or, if one has to live in the same household with the offender, would it not be prudent simply to ignore the offense and live as if it never happened?

David Stoop reminds us that we have been forgiven by God, and we cannot do anything less than forgive: "... It's important to remember that

70   Nancy Leigh DeMoss *Choosing Forgiveness: Your Journey to Freedom*
     (Chicago, IL: Moody Publishers, 2006) 126-130.

our ability to forgive flows out of our awareness of our own forgiveness by God. The more we understand how much we have been forgiven, the more we are able to forgive."[71]

Still another reason to forgive has nothing to do with the perpetrator, but with the one who has been offended, as Charles Stanley points out:

It is equally important to remember that forgiveness is for our benefit. The other person's behavior may never change. It is up to God, not us, to change that person. It is our responsibility to be set free from the pressure and weight of an unforgiving attitude.[72]

We forgive, therefore, not only for the sake of the Lord and the other person, but for our own freedom.

Bobbie Patterson backs this up, saying, "Serious side effects follow when we refuse to forgive another person who has wronged us or it is perceived they have wronged us."[73] Forgiving is in fact essential to enable us to love another. When someone says they just cannot love another person, lack of forgiveness may well be the reason, as Basil Redlich points out:

Not to forgive is not to love. If, then, we do not forgive, we, of our own choice, cut ourselves away from the friendship and fellowship of the Father. We must forgive not once, not seven times, but seventy times seven. This insistence by Jesus on unlimited forgiveness of our fellow-man cannot be gainsaid. He could not do otherwise in teaching the love of the Father for His children.[74]

How much Joseph understood and was conscious of these aspects of forgiveness is not certain. Again, as we have already discussed, there is little to no knowledge of Joseph's deep and abiding relationship with God, as there is with Jacob. The story of how Jacob told God that he would not leave unless he was blessed is quite clear, speaking of a very real and

---

71   David Stoop, *Forgiving the Unforgivable* (Ann Arbor, MI: Vine Books, Servant Publications, 2001) 69.

72   Charles Stanley, *The Gift of Forgiveness* (Nashville, TN: Thomas Nelson Publishers, 1991) 112.

73   Bobbie S. Patterson, *Forgiveness: An Act of Grace and Mercy* (Birmingham, AL: Woman's Missionary Union, 2001) 119.

74   E. Basil Redlich, *The Forgiveness of Sins* (Edinburgh: T&T Clark, 1937) 97.

honest relationship, but no such conversation is recorded for Joseph. The conversations between Job and God, David and God (and other Bible personalities and God) are given, but not in Joseph's case. Perhaps that is the reason that Joseph's story is so intriguing. Yet it can be discerned that such a relationship between Joseph and God existed, for had it not, the forgiveness embraced and abounding grace offered would not have been possible.

Springing from Joseph's relationship with the Lord and his forgiveness of others, the fruit of his life was grace. Consciously or unconsciously, Joseph understood the formula: *A choice to embrace forgiveness + forgiveness extended = grace to one another and mercy from God.*

There are seven characteristics that Joseph exhibited that the Christ-follower would do well to take note of and emulate. These characteristics set Joseph apart and made him an example for all generations to admire and learn from. As long as there is life on this planet, Joseph will forever be remembered for these seven characteristics:

I. JOSEPH MADE A DECISION FOR FORGIVENESS.

It is interesting how humans presume things about one another. The believer and the non-believer alike often assume that because they would treat someone in a certain manner, that is how that person will treat them. Sometimes it happens that way, but not always. Seventeen years after Jacob died, the brothers panicked. They seemed to presume that Joseph would treat them in the way they might have treated him – with revenge.

Even though the Bible relates this story, I have often believed that the brothers made up what they conveyed to Joseph in Genesis 50:16–17. Whether Jacob told them to ask for forgiveness is not certain, but they said that their father told them to tell Joseph to continue to forgive them. Some might argue my perception of this point and claim that Jacob told the brothers to ask for forgiveness, but this cannot be confirmed and even if I am wrong, I must be true to my own perception and at least offer my theory. What we do know is that the brothers *said* this request was coming from their father, and if my theory is in fact the case, it would be for the purpose of manipulating Joseph to forgive his brothers for the sake of their father's wishes. At any rate, the brothers began to wonder what would happen if Joseph stopped forgiving them, so they sent a messenger to Joseph asking him to continue to forgive them because (allegedly) *"Dad said so."*

Joseph probably could not believe these boys, and he might have said, "What's the matter with you guys? I told you way back then that I forgave you. I meant it then and I mean it now" (paraphrased).

Probably these boys remembered what their father may have told them about how Esau plotted to kill him when Jacob and Esau's own father died, as we read in Genesis 27: *"Esau held a grudge against Jacob because of the blessing his father had given him. He said to himself, 'The days of mourning for my father are near; then I will kill my brother Jacob'"* (Genesis 27:41). Although Esau never carried out the act, the family may have lived in some fear that Esau would return at any time and make good on his promise. And now no doubt these brothers thought that Joseph might do the same to them. These brothers knew all about revenge; they had not hesitated to avenge their sister's violation.

As human beings so often do, these brothers seem to have made an assumption; that Joseph's heart attitude was rather similar to their own, and that he would behave as they might have behaved. To ensure their own safety, the boys do some preventative maintenance by asking Joseph to continue forgiving them.

Joseph had extended forgiveness and had no thought of revoking that grace. He had already chosen to forgive them for the rest of their lives. Arguably at some point, the brothers *had* genuinely repented. So for Joseph to keep pouring on the fear of eventual punishment would have gone against what Joseph was led by the Lord to do. Such revenge was not in his plan or his character.

It is possible that people can exact *too much* justice on others. Punishment can be carried too far if genuine repentance has already taken place, as George Lawson points out:

If we truly repent of our sins, our sorrow and shame for offending God will not be expelled by the assurance of pardon either from God or man. But when men are mourning even for sin, they may carry their grief to a dangerous excess.[75]

Joseph did not desire for that type of guilt to be upon his brothers' heads and he did not desire to carry their grief to an excess that was beyond reasonable. He never downplayed what they did. He made it clear when he told them they meant it for harm. He knew they had once intended to kill him, and he called them out on it. However, once they had expressed repentance, he made it clear that God had a greater purpose in mind for all of them which they knew nothing of. Joseph made the choice to embrace and live a life of forgiveness, and to live that way for the remainder of his life.

It is rather amazing how the brothers play on Joseph's sympathies in Genesis 50:17 when they tell him that they are servants of God. These boys have been anything *but* servants of God, but now they are trying to appeal to his spiritual side. It is not clear if Joseph reads through this or if the boys are in fact true followers of God now. Whatever their true state, Joseph has already decided that forgiveness is something that must be done every day for the rest of his life. That is how forgiveness is embraced; by an act of volition – the will.

II. JOSEPH UNDERSTOOD THAT GOD IS SOVEREIGN.

God controls everything. This does not mean that God *causes* all things to happen, but it does mean that God *controls* all things, and causes good to come out of evil.

God is not responsible for sin. He did not cause Joseph's brothers to choose evil, but He does use even acts of evil to work out for His glory and for the good for those who love Him.

Joseph may have been the first one in history to realize that even bad things work out well when God is trusted and His principles followed.

---

75   George Larson, *The Life of Joseph* (Carlisle, PA: The Banner of Truth Trust, reprint 1998) 260.

God works out bad things to His good. If Joseph was not the first person to realize that, he was the first person who is recorded as saying it: *"You intended to harm me, but God intended it for good to accomplish what is now being done, the saving of many lives"* (Genesis 50:20). Unlike Joseph, we never seem to be able to reason this out until we come to an understanding that God is sovereign, and *all* things can be used by Him to result in a greater good. The Apostle Paul confirms this: *"And we know that in all things God works for the good of those who love him, who have been called according to his purpose"* (Romans 8:28). God's will can be the final result of any catastrophe.

III. JOSEPH UNDERSTOOD THAT GOD IS GOD AND WE ARE NOT.

"But Joseph said to them, "Don't be afraid. Am I in the place of God?" (Genesis 50:19). Joseph understood that he could not exact revenge on his brothers even though they seemingly deserved it. Even though He was God's man in God's place, he was not in the place of being God. Any vengeance would have to be a choice that God would make, not Joseph. Later, Moses would record God as saying, *"It is Mine to avenge; I will repay"* (Deuteronomy 32:35). Furthermore, Paul would say, *"Do not take revenge, my dear friends, but leave room for God's wrath, for it is written: 'It is Mine to avenge; I will repay,' says the Lord. On the contrary: 'If your enemy is hungry, feed him; if he is thirsty, give him something to drink. In doing this, you will heap burning coals on his head.' Do not be overcome by evil, but overcome evil with good"* (Romans 12:19-21).

It is true that Joseph did not know of the above verses at this time, but he understood the concept that he was not God and had no right to make decisions that were God's. The child of God should never take revenge even when he thinks that God is moving too slowly. There is an old saying, "The mills of God grind slowly, but they grind exceedingly fine." God is God and we are not.

IV. JOSEPH HAD A DEVOTION TO FAMILY.

Joseph spent the first seventeen years of his life with his father and the last seventeen years with his father. He loved his own boys and he loved those unlovable brothers. More than anything else, Joseph wanted his family with him.

Interestingly enough, it might have been sufficient if Joseph had said, "I forgive you for what you have done. You are free to purchase grain from us here in Egypt. Tell Dad and Benjamin I said hello and that all is well here. Have them come visit me some time, and Godspeed on your trip back home." That might have been admirable, but we might never have heard the story. That kind of response did not fit into the plan of God for establishing the Hebrew nation.

Joseph went to the extreme not only to embrace forgiveness, but to extend grace. He said, *"'So then, don't be afraid. I will provide for you and your children.' And he reassured them and spoke kindly to them"* (Genesis 50:21). He was not satisfied with giving them grain, being nice to them, and watching them drive out of town. He wanted them near.

There is a Psalm that says, *"God sets the lonely in families, he leads out the prisoners with singing; but the rebellious live in a sun-scorched land"* (Psalm 68:6). *The New Living Translation* is a real comfort, saying, *"God places the lonely in families ..."* (Psalm 68:6a NLT).[76] God did that for Joseph. God gave him a family of his own – his wife and sons. But when Joseph's brothers and his father arrived, God placed Joseph, who knew what it was like to feel lonely, back into his extended family as well. Families are God's gift to lonely people, and forgiveness for offenses recognizes the importance of remaining together as a family.

V. JOSEPH WAS A LIVING DEMONSTRATION OF FAITH.

Joseph knew that God's time for the Hebrews to be in Egypt was finite. *"Then Joseph said to his brothers, 'I am about to die. But God will surely come to your aid and take you up out of this land to the land he promised*

---

76   Psalm 68:6a *The Holy Bible, The New Living Translation* (Carol Stream, IL: Tyndale House Foundation, 2007).

on oath to Abraham, Isaac and Jacob'" (Genesis 50:24). Joseph would not see that day when the Hebrew nation exited Egypt. In fact, that day would not come for another four hundred years. But Joseph demonstrated his faith that there was a day coming when things believed for would become visible.

Do you ever stop to think that when we look at our life and the good things that have happened as well as the bad, the only thing that sets us apart from non-believers is our faith, and specifically our faith in Jesus? The belief that Jesus will return is what brings distinctiveness to the child of God. And if the Christian dies before the Lord's return, the belief that he will be present with his Savior is what makes living a life of embracing forgiveness worthwhile. A life of embracing forgiveness is a demonstration of the faith in Jesus and His promises that reside within the child of God.

VI. JOSEPH KEEPS HOPE ALIVE.

"And Joseph made the Israelites swear an oath and said, 'God will surely come to your aid, and then you must carry my bones up from this place'" (Genesis 50:25). Joseph's hope is a precursor to his faith; he hopes and believes that not only will the Israelites leave the land of Egypt one day, but on top of that, his own bones will be brought back to Canaan.

Joseph would actually die in exile, and although he personally did well in Egypt, his being there resulted in an entire nation of people becoming slaves for a little over four hundred years. But Joseph had hope. Thank God for people who see further than their own immediate circumstances and more than just the negative. John R. Stott paints a grim picture in light of Exodus 1:8, which tells us of a new king who came to power in Egypt, knowing nothing about Joseph:

> It was a succeeding dynasty that is meant. This is likely to have been the nineteenth, whose early Pharaohs built the cities of Pithom and Raamses, the latter as a royal residence in the Delta area, where the Israelites had settled. It was convenient, therefore, to use Israelite slave labor. And as the years passed, the bondage of the Israelites became crueler and harder to bear, until their lives became "bitter with hard labor in brick and mortar and with all kinds of work in

the fields" (Exodus 1:14). The Egyptian exile lasted altogether four hundred and thirty years (Exodus 12:40–41). What had become of God's promise?[77]

What had become of God's promise? It was still there. It was ever present in the mind and heart of God, although just a footnote from the lips of Joseph. Yet Joseph had hope, and Joseph let that hope be known, which will bring us to the final thought.

VII. JOSEPH BECAME A SYMBOL OF HOPE.

Although Genesis begins with a wedding and ends with a funeral, it is a book filled with hope. *"So Joseph died at the age of a hundred and ten. And after they embalmed him, he was placed in a coffin in Egypt"* (Genesis 50:26). Although Joseph died, was embalmed, and probably placed in a sarcophagus, there is no record in Scripture that he was ever buried in Egypt. Could it be that God planned this? Was Joseph's body, embalmed within a sarcophagus and unburied, intended to remain ever before the Hebrew people as a lasting memorial of hope? God may well have allowed this symbol of hope to remain visible; hope that someday there would be an exodus out of Egypt, and an entrance into the land that was promised.

Joseph was not buried until he was brought to the Promised Land over four hundred years later. *"And Joseph's bones, which the Israelites had brought up from Egypt, were buried at Shechem in the tract of land that Jacob bought for a hundred pieces of silver from the sons of Hamor, the father of Shechem. This became the inheritance of Joseph's descendants"* (Joshua 24:32).

You might wonder what this little part of the story regarding Joseph's burial has to do with forgiveness. One wonders if the Hebrew people ever thought about or discussed that the reason they were in Egypt at all was because of forgiveness – the forgiveness embraced by Joseph to his brothers. One might answer, "But that relocation of the family to Egypt led to slavery. Where is there grace in that?"

---

77   John R.W. Stott, *Understanding the Bible* (Grand Rapids, MI: Zondervan Publishers, Revised 1999) 59.

Grace can be extended even in the midst of suffering times. Had the family not relocated to Egypt, certain extinction was imminent. And for over four hundred years, as children looked at that sarcophagus and asked parents and grandparents, "Who is in that coffin?", perhaps the answer came, "That is our father Joseph, my child. Because of him and his forgiveness to his brothers, we have been given grace and a great heritage. Because of forgiveness, we were given the grace of living in a land not our own which saved us from starvation. And although we are slaves now, one day we will be free and go to the land that was promised us. Joseph's body will be buried there, and not here, because we are going back one day, and the body in the sarcophagus is a symbol of that hope."

CAN FORGIVENESS ENSURE OUR SAFETY?

After reading this book on embracing forgiveness and extending grace, you might now be asking the question, "But what if, after I choose to forgive my offender, he or she hurts me once again? Can forgiveness ensure my safety?" Charles Stanley gives another great word of advice:

What if the one we have forgiven hurts us again? What if the very same thing happens again? Will it make what we've done any less real? At first we will no doubt feel hurt, bitter, or angry – or maybe all three. Satan will remind us of our past hurts. We may be tempted to doubt the sincerity of our decision to forgive that person.

If this happens, it is important to remember that forgiveness is an act of the will. The initial decision to forgive the person must be followed by the faith walk of forgiveness. Standing firm on the decision to forgive that person and applying additional forgiveness, if necessary, allow us to replace the hurt and the defeated memories with faith victories. The new offenses can be forgiven as they occur without linking them to past offenses, which have already been forgiven.[78]

---

78   Charles Stanley, *The Gift of Forgiveness* (Nashville, TN: Thomas Nelson Publishers, 1991) 111-112.

There is always that possibility of being mistreated more than once, and there is no promise it will not happen. But perfect love dispels all fear and sees the good that another person *could be*. Despite Joseph's forgiveness, the brothers might not have changed; indeed, Joseph's rise to power might well have evoked intense resentment and jealousy in those brothers who were already inclined to such sentiments. There was no promise that this would not happen again, yet Joseph forgave them anyway.

In his book, *Grace: More Than We Deserve, Greater Than We Imagine,* Max Lucado talks about how the grace of God lifts the wounded back to his feet and sets him in position to be able to extend forgiveness and receive grace, and thus grant grace to others:

> Let him do His work. Let grace trump your arrest record, critics, and guilty conscience. See yourself for what you are – God's remodeling project. Not a word to yourself but a work in His hands. No longer defined by failures but refined by them. Trusting less in what you do and more in what Christ did. Graceless less, and grace shaped more. Convinced down deep in the substrata of your soul that God is just warming up in this overture called life, that hope has its reason and death has its due date.
>
> Grace. Let it, let Him, so seep into the crusty cracks of your life that everything softens. Then let it, let Him, bubble to the surface, like a spring in the Sahara, in words of kindness and deeds of generosity. God will change you, my friend. You are a trophy of His kindness, partaker of His mission. Not perfect by any means but closer to perfection than you've ever been. Steadily stronger, gradually better, certainly closer. This happens when grace happens. May it happen to you.[79]

---

79 Max Lucado, *Grace: More Than We Deserve, Greater Than We Imagine* (Nashville, TN: Thomas Nelson, Inc., 2012) 151.

This book began by asking, "Is embracing forgiveness a good thing? The affirmative is the obvious answer to that question, unless you are the one who must render the treatment." Yes, forgiveness is the greatest thing, and *especially* for the one who must render the treatment. When the offended embraces and extends forgiveness, he or she is then in a position to experience a life of grace – received from the Lord, and passed on to others. Who would not want that? Why would anyone want to live outside of that grace?

BIBLIOGRAPHY

Allen, David, "Preaching, Part 4: Learning from the History of Preaching," Theological Matters: Insights from Southwestern, Southwestern Baptist Theological Seminary, entry posted October 20, 2011, http://www.theologicalmatters.com/index.php/2011/10/20/preaching-part-4/ [accessed September 1, 2012].

Arnold, Johann Christoph. Seventy Times Seven. Farmington, PA: The Plough Publishing Home, 1997.

Augsburger, David W. Helping People Forgive. Louisville, KY: Westminster John Knox Press, 1996.

Augsburger, David. 70 x 7: The Freedom of Forgiveness. Chicago, IL: Moody Press, 1970.

Barth, Karl. Church Dogmatics. Edinburgh, UK: T&T Clark, 1975, quoted in H.D. McDonald, Forgiveness and Atonement. Grand Rapids, MI: Baker Book House, 1984.

Brenner, Athalya; Archie Chi-Chung; Gale A. Yee, ed. Genesis. Minneapolis, MN: Fortress Press, 2010.

Carlson, Dwight L. Overcoming Hurts & Anger. Eugene, OR: Harvest House Publishers, 1981.

Chapman, Gary. The Other Side of Love: Handling Anger in a Godly Way. Chicago, IL: Moody Press, 1999.

Cose, Ellis. Bone to Pick: Of Forgiveness, Reconciliation, Reparation, and Revenge. New York, NY: Atria Books, 2004.

Cosgrove, Mark P. Counseling for Anger. Dallas, TX: Word, 1988.

Criswell, W. A. Ephesians: An Exposition. Grand Rapids, MI: The Zondervan Corporation, 1974.

DeMoss, Nancy Leigh. Choosing Forgiveness: Your Journey to Freedom. Chicago, IL: Moody Publishers, 2006.

Epp, Theodore. Joseph: God Planned it for Good. Lincoln, NE: Back to the Bible Publications, 1971.

Forman, Miloš, director. Amadeus. Orion Pictures, 1984.

Goldman, Solomon. The Book of Human Destiny, Vol. 2: In The Beginning. New York, NY: Harper & Brothers Publishers, 1949.

Greidanus, Sidney. Preaching Christ from Genesis: Foundations for Expository Sermons. Grand Rapids, MI: Eerdmans Publishing Co., 2007.

Jamieson, Robert and A.R. Fausset. Commentary, Critical and Explanatory on the Old and New Testaments. Cincinnati, OH: National Publishing Company, 1872.

Jeffress, Robert. When Forgiveness Doesn't Make Sense. Colorado Springs, CO: Waterbrook Press, 2000.

Jenco, Lawrence. Bound to Forgive. Notre Dame, IN: Ave Maria Press, 1995. Quoted in Michel Henderson. Forgiveness: Breaking the Chain of Hate. Wilsonville, Oregon: Book Partners, Inc., 1999.

Jones, Marvin D. Joseph, a Man of Integrity: A Homiletical Approach. Cluj-Napoca, Cluj, Romania: Emanuel University Press, 2008.

Keil, C.F. and F. Delitzsch. Commentary on the Old Testament in Ten Volumes, Vol. 1. Grand Rapids, MI: Eerdmans Publishing Company, reprinted 1985.

Kendall, R.T. Jealousy: The Sin No One Talks About. Lake Mary, FL: Charisma House, 2010.

Kendall, R.T. Pure Joy. London: Hodder & Stoughton, 2004.

Kendall, R.T. The Sermon on the Mount. Minneapolis, MN: Chosen-Baker Publishing Group, 2011.

Kendall, R.T. Total Forgiveness. Lake Mary, FL: Charisma House, 2002.

Kendall, R.T. and Joel Kirkpatrick. Total Forgiveness Experience. Lake Mary, FL: Charisma House, 2004.

Ketterman, Grace and David Hazard. When You Can't Say "I Forgive You". Colorado Springs, CO: NavPress, 2000.

Kimball, Spencer W. The Miracle of Forgiveness. Salt Lake City, UT: Bookcraft, Inc., 1969.

Larson, George. The Life of Joseph. Carlisle, PA: The Banner of Truth Trust, Reprint 1988.

Lawson, George. Lectures on the History of Joseph. Chatham, England: W & J Mackay Limited, 1807.

Lockyer, Herbert. All the Men of the Bible. Grand Rapids, MI: Zondervan Publishing House, 1958.

Lucado, Max. Grace: More Than We Deserve, Greater Than We Imagine. Nashville, TN: Thomas Nelson, Inc., 2012.

Lucado, Max. The Applause of Heaven. Dallas, TX: Word, 1990.

MacArthur, Douglas. "General Douglas MacArthur's Farewell Speech: Given to the Corps of Cadets at West Point, May 12, 1962," MacArthur Farewell: The National Center for Public Policy Research, entry posted, n.d., http://www.nationalcenter.org/MacArthurFarewell.html [accessed October 30, 2012].

MacArthur, John. Twelve Unlikely Heroes. Nashville, TN: Thomas Nelson, Inc., 2012.

Mains, Karen. The Key to a Loving Heart. Elgin, IL: David C. Cook, 1979. Quoted in Charles R. Swindoll, Laugh Again. Dallas, TX: Word, 1992.

Meyer, F.B. Joseph: Beloved, Hated, Exalted. New York, NY: Fleming H. Revell Company, Reprint 1911.

Meyer, Paul J. Forgiveness ... The Ultimate Miracle. Orlando, FL: Bridge-Logos, 2006.

Mighell, Marjorie Holmes. Lord, Let Me Love: A Marjorie Holmes Treasury. Garden City, NY: Doubleday & Company, Inc., 1978.

Nee, Watchman. Full of Grace and Truth, Vol. 2. New York, NY: Christian Fellowship Publishers, Inc., 1981.

Nicoll, W. Robertson and H.J. Van Dyke. 139 Sermon Outlines on the Old Testament. Grand Rapids, MI: Baker Book House, 1957.

Niehoff, Maren. The Figure of Joseph in Post-Biblical Jewish Literature. Netherlands: E.J. Brill, 1992.

Patterson, Bobbie S. Forgiveness: An Act of Grace and Mercy. Birmingham, AL: Woman's Missionary Union, 2001.

Phillips, Richard D. The Masculine Mandate: God's Calling to Men. Lake Mary, FL: Reformation Trust Publishing, 2010.

Presson, Ramon and Ben Colter. Radical Reconciliation: The Journey of Forgiveness. Nashville, TN: Serendipity House, 2006.

Ray, Charles. A Marvelous Ministry: The Story of C.H. Spurgeon's Sermons, 1855-1905. London: Passmore and Alabaster, 1905.

Redlich, E. Basil. The Forgiveness of Sins. Edinburgh: T. & T. Clark, 1937.

Rogness, Alvin N. Forgiveness & Confession. Minneapolis, MN: Augsburg Publishing House, 1970.

Sarna, Nahum M. Understanding Genesis: The Heritage of Biblical Israel. New York, NY: McGraw-Hill Book Company, 1966.

Schechter, Solomon. Some Aspects of Rabbinic Theology. New York, NY: The MacMillan Company, 1923.

Shults, F. LeRon and Steven Sandage. The Faces of Forgiveness: Searching for Wholeness and Salvation. Grand Rapids, MI: Baker Book House Company, 2003.

Smedes, Lewis B. Forgive and Forget: Healing the Hurts We Don't Deserve. San Francisco, CA: Harper & Row Publishers, 1984.

Spurgeon, Charles H. The Treasury of the Bible, Vol. 1. Grand Rapids, MI: Zondervan Books, 1962.

Spurgeon, Charles H. Twelve Sermons on The Prodigal Son Delivered at the Metropolitan Tabernacle. Grand Rapids, MI: Baker Book House, 1980.

Stanley, Charles. The Gift of Forgiveness. Nashville, TN: Thomas Nelson Publishers, 1991.

Stoop, David. Forgiving the Unforgivable. Ann Arbor, MI: Vine Books, Servant Publications, 2001.

Stott, John R. W. Understanding the Bible. Grand Rapids, MI: Zondervan Publishers, Revised 1999.

Swindoll, Charles R. A Man of Integrity and Forgiveness: Joseph. Nashville, TN: Word Publishing, 1998.

Swindoll, Charles R. Joseph: From Pit to Pinnacle, Bible Study Guide. Fullerton, CA: Insight For Living, 1990.

Taylor, William M. Joseph: The Prime Minister. Grand Rapids, MI: Baker Book House, 1961.

Telfer, W. The Forgiveness of Sins: An Essay in the History of Christian Doctrine and Practice. Philadelphia, PA: Muhlenberg Press, 1959.

The Holy Bible, The New Living Translation. Carol Stream, IL: Tyndale House Foundation, 2007.

Thielicke, Helmut. Life Can Begin Again. Philadelphia, PA: Fortress Press, 1963.

Tibbits, Dick. Forgive to Live: How Forgiveness Can Save Your Life. Nashville, TN: Integrity Publishers, 2006.

Wiersbe, Warren W. and Lloyd Merle Perry. The Wycliffe Handbook of Preaching and Preachers. Chicago, IL: Moody Press, 1984.

Willmington, H.L. Willmington's Guide to the Bible, Vol. 1, Old Testament. Wheaton, IL: Tyndale House Publishers, 1986.

Zodhiates, Spiros. Immorality: Can We Sweep It Under the Rug? Chattanooga, TN: AMG Publishers, 1992.

ABOUT THE AUTHOR

DR. DAVID KING has pastored churches in Texas, Virginia and Oklahoma and has had extensive Christian radio management experience. He is a Biblical researcher, holding both a ThD and a PhD who has been an advising and adjunct professor at a seminary in Fort Worth, Texas. He has also toured the Holy Land and traveled in parts of Africa and China.

Dr. King works with pastors and churches of various denominations and non-denominational churches. He holds speaking, teaching, and preaching engagements, fundraises, and trains pastors and lay people in global hub-church planting and multiplication.

Currently, he is Vice President of Training for Harvesters Ministries – a global church-planting ministry based in Johannesburg and Cape Town, South Africa, focusing on church planting, pastoral training and Bible distribution. David's efforts are concentrated mostly in the United States and in central East Asia.

The work of *Forgiveness Embraced* is a study to which David has virtually devoted his life, simply because, as he says, there is no person on this planet – never has been, never will be – who has not had to deal with the issue of forgiveness in some way.

"Either we have needed to forgive or we have needed forgiveness, and most of us have been on both sides of this fence at one time or another. This is an issue that has touched every human being regardless of gender, race, economic status or religion ... without exception!"

David is married to Dr. Carie S. Tucker King, a university professor of a major Texas university and a published author. They have five grown children and reside north of Dallas, Texas.

Made in the USA
Columbia, SC
03 September 2019